OTHER DON ASLETT BOOKS
FROM ADAMS MEDIA

Clutter's Last Stand, 2nd Edition

The Office Clutter Cure, 2nd Edition

Pet Clean-Up Made Easy, 2nd Edition

Is There Life After Housework?, 2nd Edition

DONE! How to Accomplish Twice as Much in Half the Time!

DO I DUST OR VACUUM FIRST?

2nd Edition

Answers to the 100 toughest,
most frequently asked questions
about housecleaning

Don Aslett

America's #1 Cleaning Expert

Adams Media
Avon, Massachusetts

Published by
Adams Media, an F+W Publications Company
57 Littlefield Street, Avon, MA 02322. U.S.A.
www.adamsmedia.com

First edition copyright ©1982 by Don Aslett.
Originally published by Writer's Digest Books, 1982.

ISBN: 1-59337-331-7

Printed in Canada.

J   I   H   G   F   E   D   C   B   A

Library of Congress Cataloging-in-Publication Data
Aslett, Don
Do I dust or vacuum first? / Don Aslett.— 2nd ed.
        p.   cm.
ISBN 1-59337-331-7
1. Housecleaning. I. Title.
TX324.A758 2005
648'.5—dc22
2004026397

This publication is designed to provide accurate and authoritative information with
regard to the subject matter covered. It is sold with the understanding that the pub-
lisher is not engaged in rendering legal, accounting, or other professional advice. If
legal advice or other expert assistance is required, the services of a competent professional person should be sought.
—From a *Declaration of Principles* jointly adopted by a
Committee of the American Bar Association and
a Committee of Publishers and Associations

Many of the designations used by manufacturers and sellers to distinguish their products are claimed as trademarks. Where those designations appear in this book and
Adams Media was aware of a trademark claim, the designations have been printed with
initial capital letters.

Cover illustration by Tad Herr.
Interior illustrations by Christine Tripp,
with additional illustrations by Ryan Roghaar.

This book is available at quantity discounts for bulk purchases.
For information, please call 1-800-872-5627.

Introduction

Ladies and Gentlemen–
Start Your Vacuums

ADMIT IT. No one—except for mothers-in-law, and they're lying—really loves to clean. But there is help! This nitty-gritty guide gives the lowdown on the best way to clean up, making even the most unwelcome chores practically painless. Inside, you'll find the answers to such housecleaning problems as:

- Getting pet hair off everything
- How to clean miniblinds
- Banishing those reappearing carpet spots
- Attacking even the grungiest bathroom tile, and more

Filled with first-rate advice from America's top expert in cleaning, *Do I Dust or Vacuum First?* shows you how to make a clean sweep of things and earn more time for yourself.

Don Aslett, Why Does Everyone Ask YOU the Cleaning Questions?

I cleaned thousands of homes professionally in ten years of working my way through Idaho State University. And for the last forty years, I've handled cleaning problems in thousands more homes—plus millions of square feet of commercial buildings—across the U.S.A. I've raised six children (had six teenagers at once!) and faced all the real-life challenges a home cleaner does. And I now head one of the major cleaning firms in the country, Varsity Contractors, Inc. I've written more than a dozen books on cleaning, and you can hear me on the radio and see me on television helping people with their cleaning problems.

Some people call me the best, *America's #1 Expert* on cleaning. Well, I do know a lot and have done a lot, but there are hundreds of you who know how to do certain things better and faster than I do. (When you analyze "expert," you realize that "X" is an unknown quantity and "spurt" is a drip under pressure.) Though I've answered even the toughest questions in these pages as fully as possible, my answers aren't the end of the line—the final word—there will be a better answer someday!

✔ Although I'm not the be-all and end-all of household wisdom, read these answers with an open mind (all the way to the end!) and you will learn something helpful (even if it's what **not** to do).

After fifty years of cleaning homes and businesses, I realize there are situations that have no simple, neat, "revolutionary" answer. There are some real stumpers, to which the answer is just what you thought—i.e., it's a tough, tedious job, and there's no magic tip, no presto super-duper solution: "How do you clean down pillows? . . . How can I get my kids to clean up their rooms? . . . How do you fold fitted sheets neatly?" These are problems to which there is no easy, comforting answer—but there *are* answers to most cleaning problems, I assure you! Even if the answer has to be, "Have a professional do it" or "Ditch it and buy a new one." Lack of knowledge to solve a cleaning challenge is not the big problem: lack of ambition, nerve, or the time or money to proceed is usually what leaves a cleaning mystery unsolved.

I've gathered the questions in this book from all the home cleaners I've met in my travels, my professional work, more than 5,000 media segments, and my personal life. At the house-cleaning seminars I give and at other personal appearances across the country, and in the mail and e-mail every day, new questions come. We chose 100 questions for the original book because we thought those were the ones home cleaners most needed the answers to, and they were the ones asked most often. They were also questions you can't find the answers to anywhere else. We even threw in a few "rhetorical" questions to help boost morale in the never-ending war on dirt. This second edition has completely updated the original answers technically and we've even thrown in a few extras (and gotten rid of a few obsolete ones)!

If you have a burning question not addressed in these pages, please send it to me so I can be sure to consider it for the next edition. Send it to: Don Aslett, P.O. Box 700-DV, Pocatello, ID 83204.

Should I Dust or Vacuum First?

First, if you put the right kind of mat at all the entrances to your home **(see page 97, question 41)**, you'll cut dusting and vacuuming in half. Once your matting is down, always DUST FIRST!

Boo! Hiss! Snort! Argue! "If I dust first, then vacuum, it blows dust on everything I've dusted," says Vera Vacleak, Dust Bowl, Arizona. If your vacuum is in that bad a shape, you're wasting your time dusting *or* vacuuming. A good vacuum with a decent bag and tight clamps, gaskets, and seals won't leak and spew dust over cleaned surfaces. When you can *see* "resident dust" (it causes that dusty, burning smell when you turn your vacuum on) shooting out, you know your bag's too full.

✔ A vacuum has to be maintained. If you empty or change the bag frequently, you'll spend a **little** time emptying it or slipping in a new one instead of **a lot** of time wondering why the vacuum isn't picking up like it used to.

There are new types of bags available now, for both upright and canister vacuums, which do a much better job of keeping fine dust particles from being spewed back into your home's air.

The bagless vacuums shouldn't release dust back into the air, either, though some of them do (you can see it collecting even on the vacuum itself after a while). And you need to be careful when emptying a bagless vacuum's dirt cup, or dirt and dust can be spilled back into the air and on the floor. If you have a bagless vacuum, read the owner's manual and perform any maintenance it calls for (such as changing filters) faithfully. People tend to think that because a vacuum has no bag, nothing needs to be done for or to it, ever!

Dusting is more than picking up minute particles of lint or airborne residue on a picture frame. *Dusting* is brushing dirt and dead bugs off windowsills; wiping up eraser rubbings and food crumbs that missed the napkin; getting all the orange peels, gum wrappers, and taco chip fragments, as well as the toothpick ends cleverly hidden around the lamp by the sofa. If you vacuum first, all this ugly litter ends up on your freshly vacuumed floor. (Ugh!)

I've heard a lot of Vacuum-Firsters argue that even a vacuum in good working order blows dust and dirt off undusted or forgotten areas onto dusted ones. Well, get *rid* of undusted or forgotten areas—use your imagination. Close or glass in that dusty area, or find a way to rig your duster to get it.

You always want to pick up and capture the dust, not spread it around. Microfiber cloths, disposable Masslinn cloths, and lambswool dusters (see **Glossary** at the back of this book) do a great job of this because they grab and hold the dust. And with a lambswool duster on an extension handle, you can do high dusting without a ladder or stepstool.

What Should I Dust With?

First, you shouldn't be dusting much. A great deal of dust comes in on and is moved around by people, so mat your doors well **(see page 97, question 41)**. I'd also check your home's weather stripping, clean or change furnace filters, and vacuum regularly, and there won't be much dust.

Second, *cheap* feather dusters and oil-soaked rags are out. They create more problems than the original dust—rinky-dink feather dusters and blower attachments on a vacuum just move the dust around, and oily rags leave a sticky surface to attract and hold dust. **Real ostrich feather dusters (such as those made by Texas Feathers), however, work great!** Professional dustcloths such as Masslinn cloths (though they're really paper, permeated with a tiny bit of "dust treat") are pretty good. So are microfiber cloths, dry or dampened with water. Either of these will catch and hold the dust, not just scatter it. Ledges, door tops, exposed beams, the tops of tall pieces of furniture, etc., are often rough and will catch and snag your cloths, so I recommend you smooth areas like these with a light sanding and a coat of polyurethane, varnish, paint, or whatever matches the existing surface.

In some situations, the most effective duster is the dust brush of a vacuum with a good filter bag. A properly working vacuum, like the right kind of dustcloth, will pick up and collect the dust, not disperse it.

The fastest, most effective light dusting in high places is done with a big wool puff (it looks like cotton candy on a stick) called a lambswool duster. You can get these at janitorial-supply stores, and the best of them are made of real lambswool. They catch and hold dust by static electricity, and do a super job on uneven surfaces like moldings and blinds, too. You can get one with an extension handle for extra-high dusting.

A water-dampened cloth is an okay dust collector for the tops of windowsills, rails, or shelves. If the cloth gets too loaded up, it will leave wet dust behind, which comes back to life when it dries! So rinse out the cloth whenever you need to.

✔ Your object is to pick up the dust, not to knock it from one place to another, and not to leave an oily film that will attract and hold future dirt and dust.

How Do I Get Black Marks off the Wall?

Black marks generally fall into the categories of artwork (felt-tip markers, crayons, pencils), club marks (from broom handles and baseball bats), rub marks (from chair backs and furniture too close to the wall), lean marks (from things like skis and mops), and bumps (from furniture and acts of everyday living, even—gasp!—carelessly wielded vacuums).

Don't overestimate the size of a mark and make a headlong dash to remove it at all costs. Too many times, a tiny black mark on a nice enamel wall causes the homeowner to go into hysterics and—as he or she learned from the latest "Helpful Hint" book—grab some toothpaste or peanut butter and rub not only the black mark, but the whole general area.

Both of these agents do much more than take out black marks. They are abrasives and will leave a large dull spot that's usually more noticeable than the original mark. (Besides, peanut butter is too expensive to clean with!)

What is the right way to get rid of black marks? First (after you've hidden all the felt-tip markers), examine the mark and try to determine if it is removable. Most markers will come off a well-varnished wood or gloss paint surface. But remember that felt-tip marker dyes vary so much in their chemical makeup, that there is no one magic remover. Sometimes markers stain; sometimes the ink just lies on the surface. If the mark is on unsealed wood or some other porous surface, all the rubbing and scrubbing you can manage isn't likely to fully remove it.

If it seems to be cleanable, dip a corner of a clean cotton terry or microfiber cloth in a solution of all-purpose cleaner (see **Glossary** at the back of this book) and rub *the mark only*—not a six-inch-square area—gently with the tip of your finger behind the cloth, the object being not to damage the paint finish or surface. Press harder only if necessary; then buff with a dry part of the cloth. If only a slight shadow remains, leave it. If you think the mark will bother you more than a tiny dull area, dip the wet cloth in a little mild abrasive cleanser and rub lightly just on the exact area of the mark—this will take out the mark and only a little of the surface. **Make sure that any scrubbing cloth you use on marks is wet, which will help keep the surface from being scratched or abraded.**

If the spot doesn't appear to be cleanable, touch it up with the leftover paint you were smart enough to save a little of. Use a little artist's brush and feather the edges. It may stand out like a sore thumb at first, but before long it will blend in. If the stain still bleeds through, apply a stain sealant such as KILZ and then repaint.

If the problem spot is on wallpaper, glue a piece of paper from your leftover roll over it (slightly larger than the spot and craftily chosen to blend it with the existing pattern, if any). Few observers will ever detect it.

✔ When it comes to marks, face the fact that if you have children, grandchildren, or other frequent visitors who are a constant threat, you must provide a wall surface that can be cleaned.

Flat paint, elaborate fabric wall covering, wallpaper, unfinished wood, and the like are always going to come off badly from a tangle with markers. Gloss or satin enamel, plastic laminated paneling, and sealed wood surfaces all resist spot and stain penetration and are much easier to keep looking sharp.

How Do I Clean Chrome and Keep It Looking Good?

Chrome is an easy surface to clean, but it often looks bad when you're finished. This is because any cleaner residue left on the surface will dull it. Wherever chrome lurks, use a fast-evaporating alcohol-based glass cleaner (such as Windex) to clean it.

The secret is to use a dry cloth to give it a final polish after you clean. Most people use either a damp rag or an oily one, and because of chrome's intense reflective quality, every smear is exaggerated. A soft dry cloth, especially a microfiber or cotton cloth, will buff, polish, and nicely brighten up the freshly cleaned surface.

After it's clean, the way to keep household chrome looking good is to keep it dry and dusted, or every little particle and print will show. (If this sounds impossible, it probably is.)

✔ It also helps to clean chrome more often than every six years, so scum and hard water deposits don't have a chance to build up.

My nonacid bathroom cleaner will safely remove any hard water minerals or "crud" that have accumulated. Rinse the surface well after cleaning, and then polish it dry. **Wet white nylon scrubbing pads are aggressive enough for many tough deposits.**

For chrome exposed to outdoor pollutants (such as auto chrome), use a good chrome polish according to directions. Just remember that, like all metal polishes, it removes a little of the surface each time you use it. Cream chrome polish does a nice job on car chrome and mag wheels, but it's a lot of work. Do it if the "high shine" means that much to you.

What's the Best Way to Get Rid of Cobwebs? Is There Any Way to Prevent Them?

A dustmop lightly treated with professional dust treat (see **Glossary** at the back of this book) or a damp towel on a broom head will pick up the webs efficiently. Webs will cling to damp surfaces and can thus be gathered, instead of being knocked loose and allowed to float onto something else.

A well-known exterminator remarked to me, "I've never seen a house that was spider- or mouse-proof." It's almost impossible to keep spiders out. They migrate into the house (generally through cracks in the foundation and house base plates—where the house attaches to the foundation), and once in, they usually like it. A consistent spray program around the base of the exterior foundation will help if you want to spend the money. Or you can seal every crack and tiny hole in your dwelling.

Pick your cobwebs when fresh, and it will go easy and fast. If you let them hang, five coats of grease will settle on them and magnify the problem. Cobwebs can appear overnight, so you aren't a "bad cleaner" if you have a few around.

A lambswool duster is super for cobwebs—get one with an extension handle, and don't forget to dust the bottom two feet of the walls (a real dust collector)!

Lambswool dusters are available at your local janitorial-supply store or by mail order (see **Glossary** at the back of this book).

What Is the Best and Easiest Way to Clean My Mini- or Venetian Blinds?

The easiest way is the best! But before I share my wisdom, let me share a bit of history. From the 1950s to mid-1960s, Venetian blinds were a big part of my company's cleaning schedule in homes and commercial buildings. I invented a massive blind cleaning machine that failed, visited car washes (they do a bad job), and tried the bathtub caper (which most of us try at some point!). I ended up cleaning more of me than the blind. The old cotton glove trick was terribly slow and sloppy. Around 1965 (because no one knew how or wanted to clean them?) blinds seemed to disappear! Between 1967 and 1975 I was called to clean nary a single blind, so I dismissed it as a forgotten art.

But like every clothing style we struggle with, the blind came back in a big way, as the mini-blind. They're made of plastic, metal, wood, or fabric, but still, because of the horizontal slat design and the fact that they're located at the window, blinds get dirty fast. Once they're up, they soon accumulate a coat of that same sticky stuff that gets on top of the

fridge! **Cleaning one slat at a time while the blinds are in place is slave labor and generally does a streaky-poor job.** Again, car washes only mangle them, and if you've tried the bathtub, you know that's not the easiest or best method.

To maintain blinds: Dry-dust them on a regular basis with a lambswool duster (see **Glossary** at the back of this book). By closing the louvers first, you can dust a flat area instead of cleaning them slat by slat.

When you find blinds sticky, flyspecked, and coated with a film of dirt, it's time to do more than dust—it's time to wash them. *First,* do them *all* at one time if you can (and never while they're up!). *Second,* before you take them down, adjust the blinds to wide-open (so the most light can come through); then pull the cord so the blind goes all the way to the top. Then you can release the fastener clamps and remove the blind from the window mount.

✔ Be sure to wrap the cords around the blind so you won't trip on them or catch them on something during handling.

Find a hard surface, preferably slanted and preferably outside, such as a concrete driveway or patio. Lay an old carpet or quilt or canvas tarp down on it so that the blinds won't scar. Before you place the blinds on the cover, hold them at the top and adjust the slats to the utmost vertical position (so they lie flat). Lay the blinds on the cover and then take a soft-bristled brush, dip it in a good grease-cutting solution such as ammonia or Soilmaster, and scrub, being sure to get back under the cords. The first side will come clean in a few seconds. Your padding material (carpet or quilt) is now saturated with water and cleaning solution and will get the opposite side moist and help clean it. Flip the blinds completely over (so the other side of all the cleaned slats is showing) and then scrub the second side. Use a *little* powdered cleanser (which will have a bleaching and mild abrasive action) on the cords if they don't look clean. When both sides are clean, carefully hang the blinds on a ladder or clothesline (or have someone hold them) while you rinse the cleaning solution off with the hose. Then shake the blinds out once or twice to help prevent water spots, and let them dry.

This may sound a little awkward to do, but I assure you it isn't. I can clean blinds six times faster than any other method this way, leaving them grease- and film-free—like new.

P.S. Vertical blinds don't catch dirt or grease as readily and stay clean longer.

What Do I Do about a Dirty "Unwashable" Acoustical Tile Ceiling?

You have several good alternatives to replacing your acoustical tile ceilings. My favorite is the dry sponge. **A dry sponge is a flat rubber pad that acts as an eraser and actually absorbs dirt from the surface when rubbed across acoustical tile.** It is an extremely fast and unmessy tool to use. Keep swiping the sponge across the tile until it gets dirty and seems to not be removing any more dirt, then switch to a cleaner part of the sponge and keep going. When it's black all over, throw it away and start again with a new one. You should be able to get dry sponges at paint and hardware stores (also see **Glossary** at the back of this book). Acoustical tile can be easily and permanently damaged beyond most ordinary cleaning means by the combination of airborne grease and oil, cigarette smoke, water leak stains, and the sags and tears that come with time. Eventually, because of the tile's absorbent nature, even a dry sponge won't do much good.

Because soiled tile is a big problem in commercial cleaning, some people figured out a way to "oxidate" or renew the surface without using paint; we have used this system successfully in the commercial buildings we clean. Soil on acoustical ceilings is of three general types, each of which is removed separately:

1. Dirt and soot—especially around heating and cooling vents
2. Yellow-brown material—residue and tars from tobacco smoke and cooking exhausts
3. Stains from water soaking through the ceiling

During the cleaning process, the loose dirt and soot are first removed by brushing and vacuuming. The cleaning solution, which is sprayed on, contains a variety of ingredients, each of which attacks a particular component of the ceiling soil. Where does the dirt go when the ceiling cleaning solution is applied? It doesn't disappear as if by magic; rather, the dirt, having had its physical properties changed by the chemical, loosens and falls onto drop cloths below. The cleaning chemical will also loosen dirt on fixtures and grid supports and they can be wiped down.

A similar approach to this is done with a bleach spray; it does a fairly good job though the ceiling smells like a swimming pool for a while afterward. You can hire someone to bleach your ceiling, or get the chemical you need to do it at a janitorial-supply store **(page 166, see question 73)** and do it yourself. Follow the directions carefully—and be sure to cover up everything, including yourself—and you will be impressed. Be sure, too, to close the door while doing it so the mist doesn't float all over the house. If damaged or stained spots remain on the tile afterward, feather over them with a little flat white latex paint or touch them up with a little white shoe polish. If you have a lot of tile in your house, apartment, or business, check the Yellow Pages to find someone to do this for you.

When tile is in tough shape, the final recourse before replacement is to paint it. Painting will improve the overall appearance and offer a better surface for future cleaning. The bad news is that paint retards the acoustic value (and the acoustics are generally the reason the tile was installed in the first place); it also gobs in the cracks and the design or print making the ceiling look a little tacky.

If you decide to paint your tile, wash it first with a degreaser solution (see **Glossary** at the back of this book). Sponge the solution on and then wipe it off quickly with a soft absorbent cloth. Let the ceiling dry well and then brush or roll on at least two coats of semigloss latex enamel. But try the dry sponge first. It's easier!

What Is the Fastest, Easiest Way to Clean a Light Fixture?

Before starting, make sure the light is off and cooled. Don't try to clean it in place. Unscrew the mounts or fasteners. This will allow you to take down the lens and put the mounts back on the screws or bolts (nothing is worse than trying to find a tiny lost mount later, or digging one out of the gooseneck of your sink drain).

Now, either soak the lens in a sink full of hot water with some liquid dish detergent added or sponge it down with soapy water and leave it on the counter. The dirt and grime on light fixtures, especially those close to the kitchen, are tough to get off—airborne grease, deposits from cooking grease and smoke, and bugs and flyspecks that have been baked on by the bulb's heat. If you have the patience to let the lens soak so the sticky stuff will dissolve, the job will be easy. If instead you scrub

the unit, your chances of scratching the surface or breaking the lens are good. Let it soak, wipe with a soft cloth and rinse, and then let it drip dry.

If a light lens is ultradirty, soak it in a solution of degreaser such as Soilmaster (see **Glossary** at the back of this book).

If you need to wash a fluorescent lamp bulb, put on a pair of safety glasses and take it out first—I've seen too many bulbs explode or break above heads when bumped, showering eyes with glass, sodium, and bits of metal.

Lampshades (the bane of the living room cleaner) will look best if vacuumed regularly, and they can easily be cleaned with a dry sponge **(see page 16, start of question 7).** And you can clean any chrome, brass, tin, pewter, or laquered metal that may be part of a lamp unit with a spray bottle of fast-evaporating glass cleaner (like Windex). To return real metal to its original luster, you might even want to use a little metal polish!

How Do I Clean Crayon and Cement-Hard Food Out of Heat Vents?

You've probably got some old hard wax, mop strings, spider webs, and ancient lollipops or Life Savers in there, too. Grubby heat vents (floor or wall units) look terrible and are hard to clean and unhealthy—I feel better just knowing yours will be clean.

Don't try to clean them in place—it's too messy and will take too long. Ninety percent of floor heat vents can be slipped out; others might require removing a few screws. Pull the vent out and take it to a central cleaning location.

If you have a small dog, cat, or any other kind of pet or a toddler walking around, it's a good idea to block off any vent openings so that they can't get in there, and so that no one can accidentally step into one.

Fill a sink (or preferably, a five-gallon bucket) with hot water and mix in heavy-duty cleaner or degreaser and let the vent soak for a while. Most of the dirt will be released and can be knocked off with a light

scrub-brushing; if you scrub violently, you'll strip off too much of the enameled finish (then the vent will look tacky and rust). Be sure to flex the "louver mover" (if there is one) to clean around that, too. Then rinse the vent well and let it drip dry.

If your vents have been beaten up over the years, line them up on a dropcloth some day (after a good cleaning) and let them dry well. Sand off any rust and brush or vacuum the vent afterward. Then grab an aerosol can of good hard enamel spray paint and cover them well. After the paint on one side dries, turn the vents over and hit 'em again on the other side.

How Can I Get Rid of That Pet Hair EVERYWHERE?

Animal "fallout" (shed hair and dander) on floors, furniture, clothes, and car interiors is a problem for many. Some people avoid it by keeping their animals outside. The next best remedy is a good beater brush on your vacuum. Hair clings fast to many surfaces (with the help of static electricity), so ordinary attachment tools without a beater brush are slow and ineffective. The revolving brush of a beater bar will lift the hair from the surface; once it is detached from the rug, upholstery, or clothes surface, it can be vacuumed more effectively. Hand vacuums can do a good job of hair removal on things like upholstered furniture as long as they have a beater brush and are motor-driven, not air driven.

✔ A cloth lightly dampened with water will loosen hair on small areas like chair cushions so that it can be wiped or vacuumed up.

The next move is to get a "pet rake" (see **Glossary** at the back of this book). This is a hand brush that looks like a thin, miniature push broom. The crimpled bristles do a good job of gathering the animal evidence to a central location, and then you can sweep or vacuum it up. Keeping soft, inviting mats around that pets love to lie on will confine the hair to a few spots.

On clothing, the tape rollers made for lint removal, or packing tape wrapped around your hand, does a pretty good job.

Hair doesn't stick to hard-surface walls or furniture, so it easily picks up there with a damp cloth or dustcloth. Hair on hard-surface floors (a frustrating problem for many, as I know from your calls and letters) can be picked up with a dustmop sprayed with a little dust treat, or a microfiber mop. On small floors, or in tough spots like under furniture on hard flooring, a rubber broom does a great job. (See **Glossary** at the back of this book.)

When it comes to carpet, high pile hides hair better than low.

One last thought here: If you have an orange pet, you might want to consider an orange couch.

What about Those White Rings on Furniture Where a Glass or Cup Sat?

First off, don't let anyone convince you there is one miracle way to get them out. It's complicated because there are at least forty possible combinations of circumstance that could have caused the "ring burns": the furniture material itself, the furniture finish, the polishes or waxes used on that finish, the amount of heat and light (such as the sun's UV rays) the finish is exposed to, as well as the length of time the object remained on the spot. For example, a hot cup of coffee or cold drink resting on certain lacquers can cause a chemical reaction between the polish and finish—the result in either case will be a ring mark. Woods and finishes vary so much; there is just no one single method.

Strangely enough, sometimes if you leave the ring alone, the light and temperature of the room will cause the surface to "heal" itself. (A little prayer may help, too.) Light rubbing with a mild abrasive mixed with a lubricant, such as paste wax and grade 0000 steel wool, or plain ol' white toothpaste and water, may get rid of it. If it doesn't, you can try a stronger abrasive such as automobile polishing compound and water, but that's risky, depending on the finish. Whatever you use, go slowly and carefully, rubbing *with* the

grain of the wood until the spot blends in with the surrounding area. **Never rub polished furniture with a dry abrasive or it will dull or scratch the rubbed spot.**

After the treated area is good and dry, apply some furniture polish or wax over it.

If you still have a problem, wash the surface with a mild all-purpose cleaning solution, dry it with a cloth or towel, and wait a few days. If it doesn't go away, call a local wood refinisher . . . or move the flower vase over it.

How Can I Clean Behind and Under Appliances and Heavy Furniture?

Areas behind, under, over, and in back of are generally nondepreciable surfaces—in other words, dust, grease, and grime aren't hurting anything if they stay, as long as you can't see or smell them. Of course, knowing the dirt is there (whether it's visible or not) makes you feel guilty for not cleaning it (plus the fact that those areas can provide excellent reproductive environments for bacteria, bugs, mice, and their relatives). And too much dust and debris buildup around belts, motors, vents, and pilot lights can be a fire hazard.

First, use good judgment. Vacuuming in place is almost impossible, unless you've got a flat, two-foot-long "hypodermic" vacuum attachment. (If you do any vacuuming or other cleaning behind an appliance, be sure to unplug the appliance first! Dinging around with a damp cloth in back of electrical appliances can be fatal—don't do it!) Some brush manufacturers make a radiator brush that looks like a yardstick with bristles. This is great for getting the "fur" and dust: It can get down the side, under, and in back of most appliances. You can also try wrapping a Masslinn dustcloth or a microfiber cloth (see **Glossary** at the back of this book) around a yardstick to reach in back and under immovable appliances.

If you must pull an appliance out to clean behind it, remember these items are heavy and awkward for even the strongest of us, and one bad drag or pull can gouge a permanent mark in walls, floors, or furniture. **Some appliances also have short cords or pipe attachments that restrict manipulation, so be careful not to yank something loose.** If you have to pull an appliance out and it has no casters, always lift the front before you start and set the bearing points of the legs on a thick doubled towel or anything else that will slide easily and not mar the floor. Better yet—get help!

What Are the Most Dreaded and Favorite Housework Tasks?

Judging from comments I've had from the millions of people in my audiences over the years, people are always interested in expressing their feelings on this subject. They also like to find out how others feel about certain household jobs. I've received a lot of input on "favorite" and "most dreaded" housecleaning work from the comment cards I pass out at my seminars and workshops, and from calls, letters, e-mails, and conversations. The answers have had a certain amount of consistency over the years.

Favorite (after turning on the dishwasher, hiring a maid, and being through):

Number One (at least twice as popular as Number Two): *Vacuuming*

Number Two: *Washing clothes*

Number Three: *Cleaning the kitchen*

Most Dreaded (this list is more lengthy and opinionated):

Number One: *Bathrooms*. The average homeowner dreads bathrooms (and toilet cleaning) above all. No real surprise here!

Number Two: *Dusting*

Uncontested Number Three: *Cleaning blinds*

The first two items on the "Most Dreaded" list above, by the way, are obviously a real case of love/hate relationship. Though many people voted bathroom cleaning and dusting their most dreaded chores, there was a strong minority of dusters and "can cleaners" who clearly loved those tasks. Doing the dishes seems to fall into this category, too. Though many home cleaners cited it as their favorite (and no, it wasn't just those who had dishwashers), a healthy number also gave it a resounding thumbs-down.

I don't know if these statistics offer any comfort (it might help to know you have company in your hidden housework feelings—both joy and misery love company). And bear in mind that dread can be reduced by that magic word "help," be it from kids, a partner, or a professional.

Before I leave this subject, let me share a few of the respondents' most colorful comments about some of the top contenders.

Vacuuming:

"There is such satisfaction in hearing dirt get sucked up through the hose, and seeing the pile stand straight and tall again. It's like bringing the room to life."

"It's the instant gratification and visible improvement that does it for me."

"I love to see the lines in the carpet left by the vacuum."

"There's something about backing out of a clean room with just a few slight vacuum marks on a clean carpet that makes me so happy. Crazy, huh?"

Laundry:

"My favorite is laundry. It doesn't take very much energy to start the machine!!!"

"I LOVE doing the laundry. There's nothing like taking a bunch of stinky, wrinkled clothes, stuffing them in the washer, then the dryer, and folding soft, fluffy, good-smelling clothes."

Cleaning the Kitchen:

"We all spend so much time there, it's nice to have it clean and orderly. The kitchen is the heart of the home, you know!"

"I love it when the counters shine, sink gleams, etc. Makes the whole house seem clean, even when it's not quite."

"I love cleaning the kitchen because there is just something comforting and good-feeling about having a nice sparkly kitchen."

Bathroom:

"I hate cleaning the bathroom . . . YUCK!"

"My least favorite job is the bathrooms. We have three bathrooms and three boys. Need I say more?"

"My least favorite is the porcelain throne, the toilet."

"I wish I could hire someone to come in and clean only my bathrooms."

"There's nothing like the feeling of standing back and looking at a sparkling, clean, shiny bathroom when you're done. A clean bathroom is the real test of a home cleaner!"

Dusting:

"I live in a farming area on the Eastern shore of Maryland, and you can dust and 15 minutes later, you can't tell you've dusted at all."

"We have an old home on a dirt road and a lot of knickknacks, and my worst chore is dusting."

"My least favorite is dusting. BORING!"

"When my mom was giving out chores I would always beg for dusting."

Dishes:

"My worst chore is dishes. The sink fills with dishes as soon as it's empty. I HATE it!"

"If I get the dishes done, my day is off to a good start. It doesn't take long and makes such an improvement in how the kitchen looks."

"I don't mind doing dishes—my sink overlooks a rose garden and a butterfly garden and doing the dishes gives me time to think."

"My favorite housecleaning chore is all the ones the kids do . . . just kidding."

Are There Really "No Wax" Floors Now? What about Those Laminate Floors?

When we hear the words "no wax," the first thing we think of is "no wax" vinyl flooring. But a no-wax vinyl floor is about like a no-wash dish! The extra-thick protective clear layer on top of most flooring that promises to be no-wax provides a very shiny finish when new—but the "no-wax" label is misleading. Unwaxed vinyl isn't going to look good indefinitely. Sand, grit, and other abrasive particles that adhere to or embed in footwear will be carried inside and scratch and damage any surface that doesn't have a protective coating. Studies have shown that finish on a no-wax floor will perhaps last a little longer than the finish on a regular vinyl floor, but wear will eventually dull it. Dullness is not only a loss of the reflective finish; it generally means wear is now grinding away at the floor material itself.

Many vinyl floor dressings are much like whitewashing a fence—they improve the look but do little protecting. Instead of "dressing," keep your floor coated with a good acrylic floor finish such as Top Gloss. Apply finish heavily in heavy traffic areas, but to avoid buildup, don't overdo it on the edges of the floor, under the furniture, or other little-used places. Do this and you can accurately rename your "no-wax" floor a "no-wear" floor. An added bonus is that floors coated with finish are actually safer, and *less* slippery!

More than two million homes (and more every day) have laminate floors. **This is the first truly "no wax" floor. The surface of laminate floors like Pergo is so strong, dense, and tight, it keeps a handsome sheen indefinitely.** You never need or want to use a wax or floor polish on them.

The hard, compact surface of these floors will resist most soils, and what does stick to them can be removed with a cloth or mop only lightly dampened in plain warm water or, for heavier soil, a solution made with a half cup of ammonia in a gallon of water. Here is one case where you don't want to use soap or detergent of any kind, because it will leave a dulling residue behind. Many of even the toughest stains can be removed with acetone or denatured alcohol used according to directions.

Your dustmop is the best maintenance tool here—and you don't need dust treat! Don't ever use a vacuum with a beater or roller bar on laminate—that beater can strike the floor so hard and fast it will damage any floor.

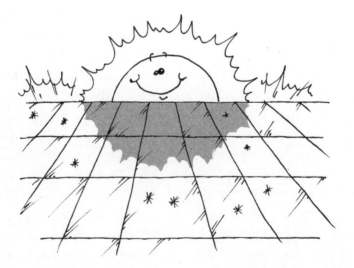

Laminate floors resist fading, stains, and damage—even high heels and cigarette burns. We are talking about normal use and wear, however. Tough as they are, you don't want to drag grand pianos across them, use harsh powdered cleansers or steel wool on them, or put sharp furniture legs on them unprotected.

✔ Chewing gum and candle wax will stick even to a laminate floor, but they can be removed easily with a plastic scraper. Dampen the area to be scraped first to lubricate the scraper so it won't scratch or injure the floor.

Laminate floors are so durable, forgiving, and easy to clean that they kind of encourage their own worst enemy, which is a neglectful owner. Because we are busy, and that beautiful pattern in the laminate will hide dust and dirt and sand and even a little gravel, we often wait until we can see the dirt or feel it underfoot before we sweep, vacuum, or dust mop it away. It takes just seconds to run a vacuum or dustmop over the floor, and in a heavily used floor area, just watch how much invisible dirt will come off. This is dust and debris that under the weight and pressure of foot traffic will gradually damage even a diamond-hard floor. You don't wait to bathe until you start smelling bad, so don't wait for your floor to look like a miniature obstacle course before sweeping it.

15 ?? ? ? ?

How Do I Get That Sticky, Greasy Dust Off the Top of the Refrigerator?

Elementary! Spray or sponge on a solution of heavy-duty cleaner/degreaser. Let it sit on there for a few minutes to break down the greasy film, then wipe it off. If the grime rolls off in little balls, it means you've waited too long to clean it and the chemical action of your soap or detergent can't handle the thickness. **Clean it more often and it will wipe off much easier and quicker.**

If the stuff is *really* scummy, use a disposable cloth or paper towel for the first wipe. Always wipe the surface dry after it's clean.

16 ? ? ? ? ?

How Good Are Those Hand Carpet Sweepers?

A carpet sweeper like a Hoky is a nonelectric, hand-powered tool that looks like an anemic upright vacuum. With a pass or two over the surface, it can whisk litter from the carpet or floor. Carpet sweepers are like girdles: They can make the surface look pretty good but don't help a bit with the deeper problem.

Because sweepers are fast and easy to use, people who have them have a tendency to use them only—and neglect their good beater vacuum, which removes the hidden soil, sand, crumbs, and the like from the depths of the pile. The result of using just the sweeper is excessive deterioration of the rug from unseen debris below the surface. **All carpet needs regular, thorough vacuuming to keep it looking good and to extend its life.**

If carpet sweepers are used only occasionally or for emergencies (like scooping up scattered popcorn between shows or cleaning Cheerios off the carpet before company arrives), they're great. If you live in a dorm room and don't even *own* a vacuum (but still like neat floors)—go for it!

Don, I Live in a Crowded One-Room Place, How Do I Keep It Clean?

The figures are impressive as to how many of us are, have been, or will someday be in a one-room living situation—a dorm, apartment, barracks, sleep-away camp, motor-home, or room at our parents', children's, or friends' home. It's also amazing how well we can get along, for how long, in one room, if we keep it clean and organized. Otherwise, most single rooms soon look as if a tornado ripped through them.

How about a short course in single-room care?

1. **Dejunk.** This is one time and place where having "too much" simply cannot be tolerated. Single rooms seem to breed stuff, so ULOs (unidentified lying-around objects) cannot stay. Box them up, label them, and put them in storage for later when you have more room. Hide things under beds or whatever if you have to, but get them out of the way. You'd be surprised how many kinds of things can be hung or suspended somewhere, from the ceiling or walls, for example.

2. **Do it now.** Anything you use, take out, or work on—put it away *now*, as soon as you're done using it. Deal with anything not enhancing life, health, or appearance, now—not when you get a chance, but *now*. There is no "later" in single-room living, because there is no room. Be sure to

include the big three in your "put it back now" program: food, clothes, and paper.

3. **The bed.** This is often the central focus in a single-room living area, as it's used not just for sleeping but for study, organizing, and often almost like a workbench. Minimizing the covers (one sturdy quilt instead of three blankets and a spread) and making the bed immediately after use will do you and the room more good than any other single act of cleaning. You have to make the bed sometime, why not now? It will look good all day instead of for just two minutes before you use it. Plus, things like remotes and pens won't get lost in it.

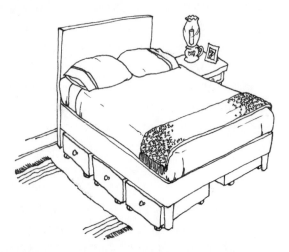

4. **Food/Eating.** Preparing, cooking, and storing food is the most frequent cause of single-room ruin. Keeping all food carefully contained (in a particular area, on or in something) is smart thinking and will prevent food poisoning, insects, odors, spills, stains, and crumbs. Never leave food out and around (or unclosed).

5. **Floors.** Since dirt and grit-carrying feet often have to pass through other areas such as hallways (where dirt is pulled off) before they reach the single room, the floors in single rooms

usually stay in pretty good shape. Keeping them policed daily or weekly by sweeping or vacuuming will generally suffice. When you borrow a vacuum, always empty or replace the bag before you return it (a code of one-roomers). If you do have a "track-in" problem, a small, inexpensive walkoff mat in your doorway will cut half of your floor work!

6. **Dusting.** Dusting isn't critical, but it does need to be done occasionally to keep dust from getting on and in clothes and electronics, etc. It takes only minutes to dust all the sills, fixtures, and furniture.

7. **Trash.** Dump it regularly—before it starts to smell or gets knocked over. And since everything on its way out is funneled through the waste containers, they do need cleaning. Occasionally, when the cans are empty, pour some hot water and a drop of dish detergent or all-purpose cleaner in there, stir it up, and let it sit a few minutes, then rinse out **(see page 135, question 58, for more on cleaning garbage pails)**.

8. **Tools.** You don't need many to do all your cleaning. One little bottle of all-purpose cleaner concentrate or dishwashing detergent is a year's supply that can generally do all your cleaning.

   - **One spray bottle filled with the diluted cleaner and water, labeled**
   - **Two terrycloth cleaning towels**
   - **Small broom**
   - **One white nylon-backed scrub sponge**
   - **A "cleaning caddy" to keep all this in (see Glossary at the back of this book)**

Keeping the single room you use, are assigned, or are renting clean says more about you and your appreciation and intelligence than a college degree or fifty thank-you notes will. It takes only a few dollars and minutes.

How Do You Clean Up Hair in the Bathroom?

Great question. It's asked by 10,000 motel cleaners and 788,520 home cleaners every day. The good news is that this hairy cleaning chore isn't that tough. A clean, damp, textured cloth (such as a washcloth) will pick hair off tub, counter, and sink surfaces easily. The trouble is, the hair on the cloth can then easily be caught or snagged by any rough surface, and as the cloth dries a little, the hair will be redistributed on other areas. Professional cleaners and smart home cleaners can dehair a bathroom in a second. They grab a couple of tissues or a few squares of toilet paper and dampen part of them slightly (not to the point of disintegration). **Hairs are generally in "flow" areas of tubs, sinks, and counters, and a few swipes with the damp tissue will collect them.** (Don't worry about mini-hairs from shaving; they just flush right down the sink, and unless your drain is badly clogged, they won't get caught.) Toss the tissue in the wastebasket and then proceed with your regular bathroom cleaning.

Here's something else that will help the problem: Install a mirror in an open area away from the sink. This encourages hair care to be practiced *away* from the sink. (Hair is less alarming on the floor or rug because a vacuum beater bar can deal with it.) Have you ever pulled out the drain stopper in your sink or tub? Then you won't have to wonder why water goes down the sink so slowly—the stopper will be absolutely hanging with matted hair and soap gunk. Stoppers should be pulled out and cleaned off regularly. Many units can be pulled from the top without tools.

Hair in sink or tub drains can be removed with a Zip-It (see **Glossary** at the back of this book), a long, flexible tool with barbs, which reaches down into the drain and pulls the hair out when it is removed.

Where Do You Start in a Closet?

You start in a closet by dejunking it. That is the simple (and often heartrending) process of getting rid of everything you don't use or need. We all know what is junk and what isn't. Dresses, pants, shirts, and shoes that haven't fit or pleased you for the last twelve years won't ever—get rid of them! Those hand-painted ties and cowrie-shell clutch bags aren't coming back in style: Out with them. Those boxes of Christmas cards from 1988, 1990, 2002, complete with address lists: Face the fact that you'll never write them. . . . etc., etc.

That's Principle Number One: Dejunk Your Closet. Once this is done, the restorative process is simple.

Move the useful but used-once-a-year (or every two to five years) stuff to a less critical (inactive) storage area. Remember, closets are your most accessible and (frequently used) storage area. Attics, under the steps, basement storage rooms, or the little shed in the backyard are not easy to get to, so transfer the worthwhile but not frequently used (passive) stuff (like camping gear, out-of-season clothes, scuba-diving masks, and suitcases) to those areas. Closets are for active, not passive, stuff.

Principle Number Two is: Get stuff off the floor. Floor mess can be the most psychologically devastating of all messes. Anything stored on a floor is prone to damage and mildew, too. Most closets have a lot of unused upper room—for a few dollars' worth of material and a spare hour or two, you can install (or barter with a friend to install) a second shelf above the one over the hanger rack.

If you are a person who rotates shoes, clothes, or gadgets for "sanitation" or style, there are pocketed wall or closet organizers you'll find useful. For that matter, there is a whole universe of closet sectioners and sorters available today. Just use your head in choosing—and installing—"storage organizers." Some are real helps; others just help you store junk higher and deeper.

Most of us may not have enough closet space (and never will), but don't pack too much into your closets. You'll defeat the purpose. No matter how cleverly you fit it all in, and alphabetize and "organize" it, if a system won't stand up to quick, convenient use, it's ultimately doomed and will aggravate the mess. Overcrowding makes it a lot tougher both to get things out and put them away. I've seen closets so crowded that hangers were unnecessary—the clothes were suspended in space by sheer compression!

> ✔ Using hard-finish, light-colored enamel when you paint will brighten the closet and make any marks on the wall easy to remove.

Finally, relax—closets don't need to be cleaned as often as the rest of the house because they are essentially concealed storage, not usually a public area even for the family, so there is some excuse for having your own closets any way you like.

There Are So Many Types of Ammonia— Should I Use Sudsy, Lemon-Scented, Plain, or . . . ?

It doesn't matter. As long as it smells like ammonia and shrivels up your hands, it's okay! I would **use plain (colorless) supermarket ammonia**—it's inexpensive and packaged in a safer dilution and more convenient container for household use. Janitorial-supply stores sell "commercial" ammonia in a stronger dilution ratio. That scares me because ammonia users are often in the habit of taking a big whiff before they use it (to make sure it is indeed ammonia), and the concentrated fumes of commercial ammonia are dangerous. Household

ammonia requires no complicated conversions to use—you just add water.

Ammonia is fairly good at cutting grease, but these days there are lots of better and less smelly and dangerous cleaners out there—heavy-duty cleaners and degreasers.

If you do use ammonia, two warnings:

1. Bleach, when mixed or used with ammonia, will create a deadly gas.
2. Ammonia, if left sitting too long on a surface, will bleach or spot (your car finish, piano top, or hardwood floor) because, when water begins to evaporate out of a 20-to-1 diluted water/ammonia solution, it becomes 15-to-1, 10-to-1, 5-to-1—and soon it is straight stuff!

21

? ? ? ? ?

My Floor Has a Design with Hundreds of Little Indentations, Full of Wax and Dirt. What Do You Think?

I think it's the pits! This is kind of like asking how to clean the ground, because old wax buildup and accumulated crud are below the surface and are not easy to get out. Even powerful scrubbing machines glide over these indentations without doing much good. **If your cleaner or wax stripper is working right (commercial stripper or mop stripper is best), it will soften and emulsify the contents of the "pits"** so, if you mop and rinse with enough water, much

of the problem will float out and you can pick it up. But you have to depend on dissolving, not scrubbing, action to get it out.

✔ Once you get the floor as clean as you can, and dry, apply a good coat of acrylic floor finish (wax). This will fill in the dimples a little and make cleaning easier next time.

Two other choices:

1. As long as it's all evenly dark: Leave it that way—few people will notice!
2. If it *really* demoralizes you, replace it.

P.S. Somebody also ought to replace the engineers who are sadistic enough to design dirt traps into a modern floor!

22

How Do I Clean Grease Spots in Back of the Stove?

Those grease bumps can get so hard that even the toughest dissolver can't work up enough action to loosen them, and they're so slick that most pads, cloths, and brushes just slide over them. **Use a "Choreperson" type (curly strand) metal scrubber with a good degreaser such as Soilmaster or a heavy-duty cleaner.** The little sharp metal edges of the pad will easily cut into even the hardest grease, and won't hurt the surface as long as it's good and wet with cleaning solution. Be sure to let the cleaner soften the grease awhile before you start to scrub—and wash your metal scrubber right away in hot water to get the grease out while it's soft.

If you have one of the newer stove backsplashes with plastic instruction panels built into it, take a gentler approach. Use a soft cloth dampened with a solution of liquid dish detergent, which is formulated for cutting grease. If you hit a particularly stubborn spot, upgrade to a white nylon-faced scrub sponge or a curly plastic strand scrubber and rub gently. Never use anything harsh or abrasive on a panel like this, never flood it with water, and never rub too hard.

How Do You Clean a Kitchen Exhaust Fan?

Dread-inspiring as they may be, hanging there covered with grease and dust, exhaust fans and other kitchen circulation vents are not difficult to clean. And it's important to do it, not just to prevent fires but because your kitchen fan or hood is a key part of your housework prevention arsenal, helping to keep airborne grease from being deposited all over.

Most exhaust fans are removable, and the first thing to do is to unscrew or unstrap the cover plate of the fan, slip it off, and immerse it in a sink full of hot water and strong grease cutter like liquid dish detergent. Now leave that to soak and look up into the exhaust opening; you'll see a grease-laden motor with a fan blade also heavy with sticky, fuzzy grease.

✔ Be careful not to wet the exposed windings and other electrical parts of the motor, and not to get moisture into any openings in the motor.

This unit is small and light and comes out easily—first reach in and unplug the cord, then lift the unit out of its motor mount and set it on some newspaper on the counter or table. Wipe the heavy grease off with a disposable cloth or heavy paper toweling, then spray some heavy-duty cleaner solution onto a cleaning cloth and use that to polish it up. Get back up on your five-foot step ladder (the ideal size for inside work), wipe out the now unobstructed opening, and clean and polish it, too, the same way.

Put the clean motor and fan unit back in the mount, plug it in, and test it by switching it on; it should work perfectly. Now go to the sink and clean the cover grill or vent that has been soaking. The solution should have released most of the grease, so it will be easy to finish up with a light scrubbing with a nylon brush. Then rinse, dry, and polish it, and put it back in place.

The procedure for vented range hoods is similar, except that most of the motors here will not be removable. Remove the grease-trap filter(s) and light lens and soak them in a hot solution of liquid dish detergent or degreaser. After they've soaked a while, change the solution if necessary and scrub with a brush, then rinse well with hot water.

If the motor is removable, unplug and remove it to make cleaning the hood itself easier. Wipe down the fan blades and motor housing as above, being careful to keep water away from the motor itself.

✔ By the way, this is a great safety measure; it goes a long way toward preventing grease fires.

Now clean the hood with heavy-duty cleaner or degreaser (make sure the degreaser you choose is safe for the finish on your hood) solution, then wipe-rinse and polish dry with a cleaning cloth. Replace the charcoal filter on nonvented units as necessary. After everything is clean and dry, put it all back together.

I've cleaned hundreds and hundreds of kitchen fans and vents; believe it or not, they take only ten to fifteen minutes. Try it—you'll be so proud of yourself when you're finished!

24 ? ? ? ? ?

How Do I Get the Stains Out of the Bottom of My Tub?

The yellow ("rust") stains you are probably referring to are also found in the bottoms of sinks and sometimes old toilets. They are generally caused by water dripping or standing for long periods of time. If they've been there many a year, you may not get them out—the minerals in the water have removed the enamel or porcelain finish or actually permeated it. Harsh cleansers and bleaches and other oxidizers may lighten stains like this a little, but will leave the area so porous that it will stain up faster the next time. Commercial rust remover, however, will often remove the yellow stain—follow the directions on the can, including all the safety precautions.

✔ Any dripping water, of course, must be stopped. Oftentimes a 25¢ faucet washer will cure the problem.

Showers, tubs, sinks, and toilets susceptible to this problem should be cleaned regularly with an acid bathroom cleaner like Showers-n-Stuff (see **Glossary** at the back of this book) to keep minerals from "setting up."

Deep, dark stains in toilets from years of hard water deposits can be removed with a strong acid solution—ask a plumber to do this.

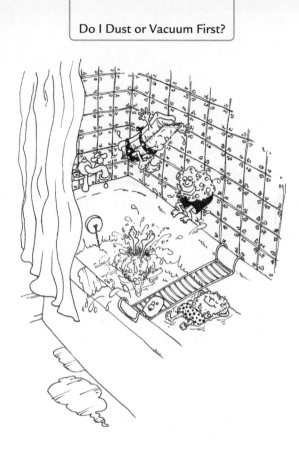

If the stain is just soap scum or hard water residue, an acid cleaner applied with a white nylon scrub pad will take it right off.

Just remember that sinks, tubs, and toilets do wear out and you cannot clean off wear or damage!

The "Routine" (Same Old Thing Over and Over) of Housework Really Gets Me—How Can I Break It?

The "routine" syndrome afflicts almost anyone doing anything, and school, art, acting, travel, romance, fishing, skiing, and writing can all become as routine as housework! We get up at the same time, eat the same breakfast, drive the same car down the same road past the same scenery. We work in the same place, and although individual situations and the people we have to deal with are different from day to day, we basically do the same thing with them, in the same way.

It's hard to get around this, the fact that having the same experience fifty times is simply not as fulfilling, interesting, or motivating as having fifty different experiences.

The answer is finding a way to turn your routine (common) experiences into uncommon, challenging ones. I think the home offers more opportunity for this than any other environment does. Here's what I do; maybe it will give you some ideas.

1. **Compete with yourself** to cut the time a routine thing takes to do. Even "fun" jobs are dull and boring if they take forever; the quicker and more cleverly we can do them, the better off we are. (Like trying to find a different, faster route home.) Things, no matter how common, that we do faster

and better than anyone else turn us on and leave the routine "drags" behind. So race the clock, don't watch it.

2. **Eliminate the routine jobs** that weren't necessary in the first place (like ironing socks, folding underwear, setting a second fork, spraying room scent and polishing the furniture every week, and washing the car twice a week).

3. **Delegate.** You have a family, friends, enterprising neighbors, youth organizations, and professional associates who could enjoy and personally benefit from some of these chores, so let *them* have them. I give most of my routine work away now—and most of the receivers who end up doing it find it challenging and refreshing because it's *new* to them. Ask guests to clean up, for instance!

4. **Make a change.** Americans work to "have it made"—to find a place and position where our lives and emotions will never again be threatened and we can live in security and ease. "Ease," defined, is simply routine, and eventually that's the very thing we end up hating! Environmental changes always bring new experiences, pressures, challenges, relationships, curiosity, and risk—and this I promise will solve the "routine blues." Try a change in your habits, work setting, schedule, tools, or associates. The change doesn't have to be *radical* (like moving to another city, buying a new house, or trekking or sailing around the world). I've seen small things like new bedspreads, visitors, taking up a new sport, going back to school, even a new time to get up in the morning, greatly change a routine—and a life.

26 ? ? ? ? ?

How Do I Get Gum Out of a Carpet?

Go to a janitorial-supply store and get a little can of "gum freeze." Spray it on the gum—this makes it brittle, and it can then be shattered into tiny pieces that will release from the carpet. A little can will last a long time and save you hours of grief. Ice in a plastic bag or dry ice can also harden the gum enough to shatter it, but it's slower and messier.

Gather or vacuum up the pieces immediately before they soften and compound the problem. The remaining residue can be removed with dry spotter (see **Glossary** at the back of this book). If there's still a spot, dip a clean towel in all-purpose cleaner solution and then wring out and rub the spot with it.

You can also pull off all the gum you possibly can, and then apply a citrus-based product called De-Solv-it to whatever is left. Use it sparingly because it can dissolve the glue backing holding your carpet together. Also it may leave an oil stain on some carpets, so it's best to test a small section under a chair, out of sight. This product works well on gummy labels as well. Because I'm a cleaner and I've seen those nasty little globs of gum all over cost companies and schools hundreds of thousands of dollars, I've come to feel that gum-chewing is ill-mannered.

Don, What's the First Thing You Notice When You Walk into Someone's Home?

I start before I get in, looking for the doormat. If there is none (or only a tiny rubber thing that trumpets the owner's name), I wince and prepare myself for the dirt in the house! I know dirt is in there **(see page 97, question 41),** so I don't have to look for any.

The first thing I notice as I *enter* a home is how used and livable it looks and feels. I'm more impressed by that than by a perfect, expensive, plushly decorated showplace. Is the music out on the piano—because it's played—or tucked neatly into a bench with an unused polished seat? **I'd rather see a cookie jar with a few crumbs around it than a gleaming sterile tile countertop.** The smell of fresh baked cookies, clean laundry, or hobby glue sure beats the aroma of "air freshener." Stains from canning fruit on the sink are a plus, not a minus, to me! **A house is made to live in, not live for!**

I notice wall decorations, too—I like to see family crafts and pictures—a Johnny van Fingerpaint original impresses me more than a van Gogh. Dust always looks worse on pretentious store-bought trinkets—miniature ships, kewpie dolls, coats of arms, and eagle plaques—than on family things. Next I listen for the concert of human interaction, young, old, and middle years—and the harmony of the music it makes.

All of these things I notice before the "cleaning" details—but have no doubt, I do get around to the physical conditions—and in the negative sense that this question is usually asked, I have three top candidates:

Number 1: Clutter, litter, and junk. These are a big part of what I notice in a home. I can accept enough dust on the coffee table to write "welcome," but I can't forget that order costs nothing (and ridding yourself of junk and clutter can even help you *make* money). Disorder and mindless accumulation not only tarnish the image of a home and its occupants, but they give me the unhappy message that the inhabitants are out of control, oppressed by their surroundings rather than served and comforted by them.

Number 2: Dingy, dirty doors. We tend to ignore doors in our cleaning, but they're actually quite noticeable and one of the first things we see walking into a house or room. You can get a lot of cleaning mileage with a little effort on your doors. Thanks to modern materials and finishes, doors are now lighter, better, stronger, and more resistant to soil and abuse. But they still get more use than anything else in your home, and believe it or not, have a real influence on the atmosphere of your home. We had a wedding reception for one of our daughters once at home. There wasn't time to do a major overhaul of the house for the occasion, so I went through and cleaned up, touched up, and polished all the doors. That alone made the house seem to gleam all over. Don't underestimate the power of your doors, or neglect the little care they do need.

The airflow through the house causes static electricity within the door casings and housings, and lots of dust and dirt will collect along the stop and hinge areas. A quick wipe will surprise you, and keep the dust level down.

A light sanding of the tops of older wooden doors, followed by a couple of coats of polyurethane, will make them quick and easy to dust (without snagging the cloth).

Doors collect a lot of little debris at thresholds—pull out the hand vac and swoop that all up. Doors also get marks and nicks from purses hitting them and people kicking them and carrying things through them (like cleaning equipment). A good once-over with a white nylon scrub sponge dipped in all-purpose cleaner will remove most of this. If that doesn't do it, it's easier than you think to deblemish wooden or painted doors, with a little fine sanding if necessary, and then a bit of stain and urethane or touch-up paint.

Number 3: The basic condition of the dwelling. It pains me to see chipped and peeling paint, and walls that reflect abuse and lack of maintenance, not normal wear.

For some reason, cobwebs don't bother me—they can spring up overnight. And you can stop worrying—dead plant leaves (on the floor or in the pot) don't bother me either.

P.S. But don't worry—since I've become a "world-famous housecleaner," no one invites me home anymore.

Are Old or New Homes Easier to Clean?

Modern building codes, engineering and design, and materials put new homes way out in front for ease of cleaning. The average new home has eight-foot ceilings; old homes have nine- or ten-foot ceilings or even taller. Woodwork and baseboard trim in new homes are plainly designed and the edges are slanted, so that dust rolls off; in old homes they are wide and often decorated with mitered grooves and flat edges that catch dust and dead flies. Windows in old homes are much more difficult to clean and maintain (and for that matter, to open); a modern house has smooth-sliding thermopane units that often can be tilted in for easy cleaning. Open fireplaces and old-fashioned furnaces, too, are dirtier than modern units, and this is aggravated by the lack of insulation in old houses: Poorly insulated outside walls make inside walls get filthy faster.

Hardware is a big time-taker in cleaning homes, and old homes have more of it. Doors in new homes—mahogany, birch, or plastic—are generally flat, smooth, and simple in design; in old homes their embossed or carved decorative trim is a pain to clean or refinish. The walls and woodwork of old homes have usually been painted so often that they look a little lumpy and saggy, even when clean.

Flooring quality and installation techniques have improved tremendously in the past thirty years, so floors in new homes are less of a cleaning challenge. Man-made fibers in modern carpet are more easily maintained than the old cottons and wools. Cellars and attics, common in old homes, weren't exactly an assist to cleaning efficiency (mainly because they offer junk storage), and dirt floors in cellars were accepted in even the finer old homes.

Bathroom fixtures in old homes are tougher than the new plastic and fiberglass styles, but they've endured years of "grinding" with scouring cleansers, which has deteriorated the surface—making cleaning harder.

All in all, new houses can be cleaned more easily and quickly. The only problem is the average new home is much bigger (thus more full of junk), so in terms of time, it's almost a toss-up. (Of course, "new" is automatically expected to be cleaner, so you owners of old homes can get away with more!)

I Have Stainless Steel Sinks and Appliances—How Can I Make Them Look Good?

It might make you feel better to realize that stainless steel isn't nonstaining steel—it stains less than plain old steel, but it does stain and it's not your fault. **Stainless steel lasts, and it doesn't rot or rust, so it is generally an attractive, sanitary, and low-maintenance home surface.**

First: Don't get overly excited, and quit swearing that you're going to paint all the stainless steel in your house! Stainless steel, especially the brushed surface found on most sinks or kitchen appliances, will soon cloud, streak, and water-spot, and slowly take on a "used" look. In other words, it stains! In some of the commercial buildings my company cleans, there are 600 stainless steel drinking fountains to clean. They are a high-complaint item, hard to clean—and once clean, their appearance deteriorates quickly.

There are many stainless-steel cleaners and polishes on supermarket shelves, most of which offer only a little help. A lot of elbow-flexing will leave the unit pretty decent, but generally as soon as you get a dribble of anything on it, that glowing surface looks the same as before you started.

I personally wouldn't *have* stainless steel anyplace in a house I wanted to look glamorous, though it's fine for the kitchen or other utilitarian places. Get vitreous china or porcelain fixtures next time for consistently better looks and easier cleaning.

If you do have stainless steel:

1. (The best approach!) Clean it thoroughly with a mild detergent solution, rinse, and buff it dry immediately with a cloth or towel, and then forget it. Learn to love the mellow, satiny look. **A damp microfiber cloth does an excellent job of cleaning everyday dirt and leaves no streaks.**

2. Some people treat stainless steel appliance panels and the like with lemon oil, waxes, silicone-type materials, or other protectors for a nice luster or "glow." It looks good, but in the long run any treated surface will require more upkeep.

3. Some professional stainless steel cleaners/polishes work well (Crème Clean is one of the good ones), and some of these are aerosols. You can get products like these at a janitorial-supply store or from my mail order catalog.

What Is the Best Way to Clean Carpet?

The best carpet cleaner by far is a combination of effective matting to keep soil out **(see page 97, question 41)** and good regular vacuuming to remove any soil that does get in. **Eighty percent of carpet soil comes in by foot traffic, and good mats at all of your entrances will keep a great deal of it from ever getting onto the carpeting.** Add regular vacuuming with a good beater-type vacuum to your matting program, and you will vastly reduce the amount of deep cleaning your carpet will require.

When your carpet does reach the point where it needs to be cleaned, first consider having it done by a professional. He or she will have the equipment and expertise needed to get out all the deeply embedded soil that damages carpet, and to take care of special stain removal problems. Most rental units don't have the power to do a good job, and most home cleaners don't have the know-how or the chemicals they need to accomplish a really good deep cleaning on their carpeting.

The best method of all, when it's available and you want a real "showcase" job, is a combination of rotary shampoo on heavily soiled areas and hot water (steam) extraction overall, with prespraying where necessary. For ordinary everyday purposes, what you want is hot-water extraction done from a good truck-mounted unit, with prespraying and prespotting for any problem areas.

Every second or third carpet cleaning, **I also strongly recommend the application of a good soil retardant** (Don Aslett's Time Saver Carpet & Fabric Protector is one) to help your carpet shed soil and stains and extend the time between major cleanings. A professionally deep-cleaned and soil-protected carpet will look nice for a long time with nothing more than the simple maintenance described earlier and occasional spot cleaning.

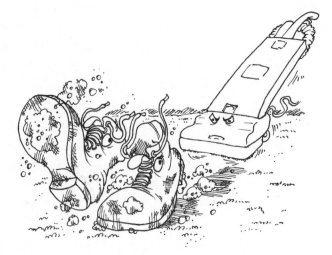

If you still insist on getting a rental unit and doing it yourself, you should know which kind of shampoo or steam cleaning solution is best. Most of the many products available do an acceptable job of cleaning—the big difference is in the type of residue they leave. Put a little of the shampoo you intend to use in a flat dish and let it dry out thoroughly. Observe how the shampoo dries. Some will leave a brittle, powdery residue that will vacuum out of your carpet easily and not attract new soil. Others leave a sticky or gummy residue that coats the carpet fibers and accelerates resoiling. When a freshly cleaned carpet resoils quickly, this is usually the reason.

As important as the type of shampoo you use is where you rent the equipment. A janitorial-supply store **(see page 166, question 73)** can rent you a more effective extractor or steam cleaner than a supermarket can. And even when shampooing carpet yourself, you want to vacuum it well first and be sure to prespray. To do this, fill a weed sprayer or spray bottle with a carpet prespray such as Pre-Spray Carpet Treatment (see **Glossary** at the back of this book). **Before you "shampoo" the carpet, spray all the traffic areas and other heavily soiled places, and then give the spray five to eight minutes to do its thing, but make sure it doesn't have a chance to dry.** This will loosen and emulsify the dirt, so that when you follow up with the extractor, it will clean twice as well.

If your carpet has been shampooed before, there is undoubtedly plenty of shampoo residue in it, so you may want to use a two-step method of prespraying and then going over the whole carpet with a rinse-neutralizer. Vacuum well first and prespray all the soiled areas of the carpet. Then fill the tank of the machine with water and add my Carpet Rinse & Neutralizer and apply it to the whole carpet. This removes all the prespray you applied, reducing the chance of resoiling. It also counteracts any chemical residue in the carpet from previous cleanings, so it reduces the chance of brown spots from pH reaction.

What Should I Do with My Wood Surfaces?

Not what you are led to believe! All kinds of oils, conditioners, lemon formulas, grain groomers, and other concoctions are foisted on unsuspecting consumers as "good for wood." Most wood surfaces (walls, paneling, floors, furniture) have several coats of a clear urethane or varnish finish over them that seals off the actual surface of the wood. It doesn't allow any of this "miracle" wood stuff to get to the wood anyway, so generally you can use the same kinds of mild cleaners on your wood that you use to clean other surfaces.

No special procedure is needed to clean wood that has a sealed finish. I've even used wax stripper on my birch cupboards—it dissolves that kitchen grease/oil slick in seconds and doesn't hurt the wood because it doesn't ever *get* to the wood.

If moisture gets into wood, it swells the grain and accelerates deterioration, and if the wood has paint or finish on it with the tiny cracks that can develop with time, the swelling will eventually chip off the finish. So it isn't wise to wet wood down (most of you know that, thus the miracle wood oils are sought). Whatever cleaner or cleaning solution you use, apply it quickly, remove it quickly, and then buff the wood dry with a soft cloth.

Older sealed wood finishes may be worn and may have developed tiny gaps and holes in the finish over time. My Wood to Wood finish will restore the full beauty and protect against moisture and stains.

On paneling, I always use a solution of oil soap, such as my Wood Wash, Murphy's Oil Soap, or Pledge wood soap. Note, I said *soap*—I use Murphy's not because the finish needs to be oiled but because Murphy's contains enough vegetable oil to make the panels shine up when cleaned and buffed, which saves application of the spray gunk polishes. Harsher cleaners won't promote a nice sheen.

Bare wood presents more of a challenge. If it has smoke stains, grease, or crayon on it, cleaning generally makes it worse. If you want to keep bare or raw wood around (if you *want* to suffer), it may need to have penetrating oil such as lemon oil applied regularly to keep it from drying out and cracking.

Wood surfaces are nice in a home; they project a homey warmth. So when you plan them, be sure to make them maintainable. **Wood that keeps you so busy cleaning and treating that you don't have time to appreciate it is stupid!** "Feeding" wood (walls, furniture, or the like) is a waste of effort and material. Many different fine finishes are available that seal the surface, and if applied right form a sturdy clear protective layer over the wood. That beautiful grain will still be fully visible, but marks and stains end up on the finish instead of in the wood. For most purposes you will probably want to use a satin or low-luster finish.

If you wish to apply or reapply a varnish or polyurethane coating on ailing wood surfaces:

1. First, clean the surface with a strong cleaning solution (a strong ammonia solution, wax stripper, or degreaser if it's a surface that's previously been sealed; solvent if it's raw wood) to remove dirt and grease.
2. Let it dry until any swelled wood grain goes down.
3. Wipe with a deglosser. This can be bought at a paint store; follow the directions on the can.
4. A few strokes with fine sandpaper should take care of any scratches or tiny bumps.
5. Then wipe with a cloth dampened with paint thinner (or a tack cloth) to pick up any lint or dust on the surface.
6. Apply the finish (paying attention to the *directions*); it may take two or more coats.

If you have any other questions, consult a good local paint store.

How Can I Enjoy My Fireplace Without Icky Soot and Ashes?

I've had fireplaces in my homes—in fact, I designed and built them myself—since we all love the idea of a "rustic, romantic" fireplace. When I learned that most fireplaces pull heat out of the house instead of putting it in, I converted the open hearths to metal inserts (wood- or coal-burning stoves that fit neatly inside a fireplace). I then had a warmer house, but still had some soot and ashes.

If your heating unit is working well, soot and ash will be minimized (and I learned this from the best— Dee and David Stoll, famous professional chimney sweeps). I've seen properly installed carousel fireplace units burn for weeks— they were so efficient only a few handfuls of ash remained.

In time, creosote and soot will accumulate in any chimney, increasing the chances of getting dirt and smoke through your house, and making you susceptible to a dangerous chimney fire or carbon monoxide poisoning. Clean your chimney, and then check the dampers (see that the opening and closing mechanism works). That's the easiest way to get "de-ickee-d." There are many professional chimney sweeps available; be sure that the one you pick is certified to inspect as well as to clean. If you are an adept roof scaler and want to do it yourself, you can purchase chimney rods and brushes (they come with directions). Be sure to seal off the bottom of the chimney before you start or you'll have soot all over your house!

Leave the damper open and do this next part of the operation in the coldest part of the day (the colder it is outside, the better the draft). Scoop up all the soot and ashes with a brush and dustpan and dump them into a metal bucket you set right in the fireplace, and most of the dust you stir up will go up the chimney instead of all over the house. Once you remove as much as possible by brushing, sweeping, or scooping, you can use a shop vac to remove any dust remaining in the cracks.

Make sure ashes are "out" before tossing them in the trash—live embers can survive much longer than you would imagine.

The surest way to enjoy a fireplace without soot and ashes is to have a gas-fired one. This is not 100 percent as romantic, but it does reduce fireplace cleaning to cleaning out the burner orifices with a pipe cleaner once a year!

Any Time-Saving Ideas for Cleaning Knickknack Shelves?

Anything full of "things" (or out of reach) takes longer to clean—that is a fact of housecleaning. If you only keep the things you really love enough to dust and clean regularly, you'll eliminate most of the knickknacks on high shelves (maybe the little kids can't reach them now, but you can't see or appreciate them much either).

Alas, there is no simple answer to the knickknack question—because there are 2,200,723,857 different fuzzy, prickly, shiny, sparkly, metallic, dull, glossy, hand-painted, hand-carved knickknacks in existence. Even some of the sturdier stuff that won't snag or break easily will often discolor when water touches it, or crumble or fade from cleaning operations. In one house I cleaned after a fire (smoke damage), there were 7,400 knickknacks. They were of good quality and we hand cleaned them in a sink. **Grease-laden washable knickknacks benefit from washing gently—in a solution of hand dishwashing liquid**—then rinsing well. Anything with a clear or shiny surface needs to then be dried immediately with a soft clean cloth.

Overall, for routine regular cleaning of knickknacks, I use an ostrich feather duster. If I'm going to handle them, I choose a Masslinn cloth, a soft treated disposable dustcloth that picks up dust and dirt and leaves the surface clean; a microfiber cloth; or even a lambswool duster depending on the size and nature of the knickknacks and where they're located. If you don't have any of these, use a damp cotton cloth.

On a large rough-textured surface with no loosely attached small parts, a vacuum with a dust brush attachment is hard to beat (as long as you keep a firm grip on the knickknack in question).

The biggest time-saver, if you are a knickknack addict, is to enclose the little charmers so they can be seen and enjoyed without worries about settling kitchen grease, cobwebs, flyspecks, and *dust*. "Enclosing" usually means a glass cover in front of the shelves—or buy a china cabinet. Or design your own ingenious enclosure.

A little hard thinking on your part will save a lot of cleaning time. Remember Don Aslett's guide for telling the difference between important and unimportant things: "Don't love anything that can't love you back."

What Is the Biggest Housecleaning Time-Waster?

Picking up litter! Too much of home cleaning is almost nonstop pickup of litter and clutter. This is not a progressive pastime, because after you're through, you're right where you should have been when you started. Solving this problem does more than free up your time: It's a great tension reliever, because you're spared the constant worry, "If someone stops by now, what would they think of us?"

Household litter and clutter also cause plenty of fights and frustration. When family members can't find something—even if they lost it themselves—everyone else has to take the blame as the seekers whine and stomp through the house trying to locate the items they should have put away in the first place. Litter and clutter cause more arguments than anything except finances and are responsible for many household accidents.

A littered, cluttered house is more visually and emotionally offensive than a dirty house because at least dirt has some natural authority, an excuse for being there. Dirt can be accepted to a degree—things get dirty with use, but household litter and clutter is just personal possessions out of control.

Litter has three general causes:

1. Your family owns too much junk (excess toys, towels, trinkets, ties, playthings, furniture, books).
2. Your home has inadequate or inefficient storage spaces—racks, shelves, closets, hooks, towel bars, and toy boxes.
3. You (the adults) have accepted the position of "family janitor" to a thoughtless bunch of litterers.

You are smart enough to cure all three; if you do, you'll cut the time you spend cleaning—and the hurtful anxieties of litter and clutter control—unbelievably.

My Formica Countertop Marks Every Time I Drag Anything Across It— How Can I Prevent This?

"Formica" is a trade name for a plastic laminate used on walls, counters, furniture, and more. A number of companies make different grades and qualities of countertop laminate. Laminates have some outstanding characteristics, including durability, stain resistance, and a good, long lifespan. Once glued down with contact cement, they are there to stay. Damage or dissatisfaction with a color or other characteristic is not easy to change or fix. **All laminates gradually lose their surface sheen as they age and wear, making stains and marks tougher to remove.**

Before you start the ambitious job of ripping laminate off, check your appliances' slide points— those small rubber or plastic tips fastened to the legs or bottom of the toaster, waffle iron, mixer, etc. Often they are the culprits leaving the marks. (If the problem is really bad, you can put

on new points, but it's probably not worth it.) I use an Armor All–like product called Dazzle to revitalize my counters (see **Glossary** at the back of this book). Choose your countertop wisely. Some colors and textures are real losers to keep looking good, especially if they get heavy use (a sad surprise to many people). Textured or matte surface laminates look rustic or homey, but mark worse and are tougher to clean than the smooth type. Patterns and flecked or marble designs camouflage marks nicely. Pure white is like wearing white pants, and you know how that goes! **Remember, countertops are something you clean everyday, one of the most used areas in the home.**

P.S. Because today's countertops are ten times better than those of yesteryear, we often think we can use them as a chopping block, anvil, or hearthstone. Sharp kitchen tools and excessive heat will damage even the best product.

How Do You Keep "Dirt Paths" Out of Your Carpet?

I call these unsightly paths angling across your carpet "cow trails," because they look as bad as where a herd of cows, one following the other, walk across a plowed field. **Cow trails are on all carpets; they are the result of wear in the traffic patterns.** Unfortunately, because of the crushing and matting of the fiber in these areas (and color change on some carpet), dirt paths show dramatically and everybody notices them.

The logical first step is to buy carpet in a color that camouflages the trails (gold, yellow, white, pastel blue, and pink are *not* cow trail–concealing colors). Any solid color carpet will show traffic trails worse than a patterned one, and extremely light or dark colors are worse than mid-tones. (Medium earth-tone tweed is probably the best for hiding dirt and wear.) Sculptured or textured carpets also help hide cow trails.

The second step is to mat your entrances **(see page 97, question 41)** to keep down the amount of dirt tracked into the house.

Third (if your carpet is in and mats are installed), is to vacuum the traffic areas better and more frequently.

An inexpensive carpet rake will help rejuvenate mashed pile so it blends in with the rest of the rug. In some cases, a plush

nylon runner mat (which could even be made of the pieces that were left over when the carpet was installed, finished on the edges) will be a dignified solution to the problem.

Now, here's a carpet-maintenance technique that cuts the need to give those cow trails a major deep cleaning. Assuming you do vacuum regularly, like you should, most dirt accumulates on top of the carpet. To keep that surface dirt cleaned off, moisten a thick terry towel with carpet-cleaning solution and run it over the carpet. It will pick up and absorb much of the surface grime.

What about Those Plastic Covers to Protect Furniture and Carpet?

I think clear plastic runners used over carpet and plastic slip-covers for upholstered furniture are the epitome of tackiness as well as real losers when it comes to maintenance and cleaning efficiency. If existing surfaces can't be used for what they were intended, why have them?

Clear plastic carpet runners are visually offensive and present two different surfaces to be kept clean instead of one. Furniture arm covers (if used) are never straight—if they're still on the arm at all. Plastic slipcovers, too, often look "slipped" or wrinkled and are never the same high quality as the furniture they cover. Why pay the price for a nice chair and cover it with a cheap-looking cover?

Plastic covers collect and *display* dust. Why deprive yourself of the pleasure of sinking down into a soft upholstered cushion—who wants to crackle down on a piece of cold plastic? You bought the chair to enjoy, not exhibit. Think about that when you're planning your next purchase, and buy what you can comfortably make use of without having to cover. I highly recommend a soil retardant for upholstered furniture (like Scotchgard by 3M or Don Aslett's Time Saver Carpet & Fabric Protector).

While on the subject, let me also address the peel-and-stick shelf paper for cupboards. This stuff is trickier than you think to apply neatly, and when you go to remove it, it leaves a sticky residue that collects lint and dirt and makes for gobby painting. Consider switching to the rubber-like shelf liner with Microban or using removable brands.

Use good enamel paint or clear finish to line your shelves—and keep them clean! You'll find that they look better—and in my opinion, it's much more sanitary.

38 ?????

When Is the Best Time to Deep Clean?

The best time to clean is a combination of when you feel like it and when things need cleaning. "House prouds" who clean by habit are wasting time and energy. These are the people who vacuum daily, dust hourly, right on schedule, sick or well, earthquake or flood—whether it needs it or not.

Try to clean every day for a few minutes instead of the once-a-week (or month) onslaught. You should clean when:

- Dirt is producing a negative situation—appearance-, health-hazard-, or human-relations-wise—and before accumulating dirt, muck, and grease begin depreciating your home.
- You are fresh and well. The majority of successful, happy home cleaners clean in the morning—that should tell you something.
- The mess is fresh. The difficulty of cleaning generally multiplies with procrastination—not only will it take more work to clean things up "later"—but it'll be harder to gather the gumption to get started.
- You are likely to have minimum distractions. Interruption, as every homemaker knows, is one of the biggest deterrents to cleaning.

Contrary to popular belief and tradition, **spring is possibly the worst time to do a heavy annual housecleaning.** This longstanding ritual may have developed because it took the beautiful spring weather to get up enough courage to face twelve months of accumulated dirt and cobwebs in hard-to-get-at places. But spring is a time to get out and enjoy the fresh earth and air, flowers, and birds—not to be cooped up breathing ammonia fumes and sorting junk.

Fall, around the middle of October (or right after the Halloween pranks) is the best time to deep clean, for both you and your house. It's cool outside, the kids are back in school, and equipment and supplies are cheaper thanks to the fall sales. But more important, dust, damaging dirt, flies, bugs, tar, and other spots and debris that enter your home during the spring and summer months should be removed at the end of the summer. Otherwise, the dirt stays around for the next eight months depreciating your house, increasing cleaning time and effort, and (believe it or not) draining you emotionally.

Spring cleaning gives you a clean house for a month or two, like April and May. Then from June through September, the heavy outdoors-use season, the house accumulates dirt and grime, which then remains in your house all winter. When you clean your house thoroughly in mid-fall, it will stay cleaner for a greater length of time—October, November, December, January, February, March, and April—and it's cleaner for three major holidays: Thanksgiving, Christmas/Hanukkah, and New Year's. Try *fall cleaning* this year and see the difference it makes. Especially notice how much longer the windows stay clean—clean windows don't last long when spring rain or a dust storm comes along.

✔ As for painting, select the driest time of year, when there's the least moisture in the air—which may or may not be fall, depending on where you live.

My Pet Has Had "Accidents" on the Carpet—How Do I Get the Odor Out?

Odor control is not as simple as the TV ads often make it sound—as you've most likely discovered. Ridding odors this way is generally masking them—or in plain talk, covering up the unpleasant odor with a stronger, more pleasant one. It's great while company is there, but later the old smell still permeates your dwelling.

✔ There are also "odor neutralizers" available, which change the molecular structure of an odor so we won't smell it. They are helpful in some situations but won't do much for old pet stains or for new ones that have sunk into absorbent surfaces like carpet.

"Get rid of the odor source" is the first step, which means clean up as much as you can of the pet piddle or poop as soon as it occurs. In the case of pet urine, put clean absorbent cloths on the spot after you have wiped up whatever is on the surface, and put some weight on them to absorb as much of the urine as you can.

Now you need to clean the carpet thoroughly. For this (and other nasty organic smells, like vomit) you need a *bacteria/ enzyme digester* such as Eliminator. (This product along with the

whole realm of pet clean-up is detailed in my book *Pet Clean-Up Made Easy, 2nd Edition*—see also the **Glossary** at the back of this book.) Many enzyme digesters need some time to work their magic of actually digesting the cause of the unpleasant odor, so be sure to follow the label directions.

Bear in mind that **when smelly liquids penetrate the carpet they often seep into the backing or pad, which is usually rubber, so it's difficult to get the smell out.** (That's also why cars, couches, etc., that are exposed to tobacco or other smells for weeks are obnoxious for a long time.) If your rug pad is permeated with odor, you should replace it.

Air circulation and sunlight have a good neutralizing effect on odors, so don't underestimate the value of a fresh breeze. Odor neutralizers such as X-O will also help eliminate bad odors from pet stains, though they may have to be periodically reapplied. If you're a dog or cat lover and for one reason or another the prospect of endless vigilance against "accidents" looms before you, I'd advise that you **use a soil retardant on your carpet before the problem occurs.** Nylon and manmade fiber carpets are less damageable (by both the original incident and by odor removal procedures). There are also special "pet proof" pads available now to resist the absorption of pet stains and odors.

P.S. A little time spent doing a proper job of housetraining your puppy initially beats a *lot* of time (and bad temper) cleaning up "accidents" later.

I Love Bleach to Clean With, Do You?

Nope! Basically, bleach isn't a cleaner, it's a powerful oxidizer. It works great in the wash because it is always well rinsed out. But just because things are whitened doesn't necessarily mean they're clean. Bleach's chemical power encourages us to think of it as a clean-all, kill-all, restore-all. **It actually isn't much of a cleaner, and is potentially very dangerous if used incorrectly.**

Chlorine bleach, used regularly (even in diluted form), will deteriorate fabrics, chrome and other metals, plastic laminates (such as Formica), and many other surfaces. Bleach combined with any acid (such as bowl cleaner or vinegar) produces deadly chlorine gas. Add to this the danger of splashing or spilling bleach on skin, carpeting, clothing, or some other surface, and the injury or expensive damage this could cause. **Leave the bleach in the laundry room, and use it only as directed there.** If you are using bleach as a disinfectant, consider a hospital-grade quaternary disinfectant such as Clear Lemon instead.

You've Said That Mats Are the Most Important Time-Saving Investment. Why?

Mats prevent housework! Remember, the first principle of smart housecleaning is not to have to do it. At least 80 percent of the dirt in your house originates outdoors, and most of this is tracked in on people's feet. Doormats can clean more dirt out of your house just lying there than you can hustling around. Where is your carpet the dirtiest? Right inside the door, on the 3' x 4' area where a mat should be. Doesn't it make a lot more sense to shake out or vacuum a mat than to chase dirt all over the house?

You should use mats both *inside and outside* every entrance to your home:

FOR OUTSIDE–AstroTurf is my favorite "preventer" of housework, my favorite housecleaning secret, my secret weapon. AstroTurf doormats do their job even when your kids don't wipe their feet. The very act of stepping on Astro-Turf puts its tiny plastic scraping blades in motion, cleaning the bottoms of those grungy shoes. Best of all, the dirt, mud, and mess won't sit on top of the mat for the next person to track in. All the muck drops down inside the mat where you can't even see it.

FOR INSIDE—Get a good professional-quality nylon or olefin mat with a vinyl back—the kind you see at the entrances of hospitals and supermarkets. These are the best all around for effectiveness, ease of cleaning, looks, lasting power, and safety. Never use scatter rugs, throw rugs, or scabby remnants.

To do the best job of dirt-catching, mats should be as wide as the door, generally three feet, and at least four strides long. These mats can be purchased at a janitorial-supply store, or from the Cleaning Center in a variety of designer color choices (see **Glossary** at the back of this book).

You've Taught Us to Clean Large Windows with a Squeegee, but How Should I Clean Those Small-Pane Windows?

In my first cleaning classic, *Is There Life After Housework?* I taught home cleaners across the country to clean full-size and large windows with a squeegee, like the professionals do—it's faster, easier, does a better job, and is even cheaper. Now what about those small-pane windows?

Don't cut your squeegee down to midget size and try to use the squeegee method—it isn't worth it and you'll get a pain out of every pane. Bear in mind for starters that these small "checkered" windows are a big window area interrupted by numerous support sills, and because of the distraction of the crisscrossing sills, they don't show dirt, streaks, or specks like a big unbroken expanse of glass would.

> ✔ Small-pane windows were designed to give a house a romantic touch, so if spiders are holding hands in the corners, don't let it worry you, it just adds to the décor!

To clean tiny windows I'd use a plastic trigger-spray bottle with a solution of fast-evaporating alcohol-based glass cleaner. (If you mix it up yourself from concentrate it will be much

cheaper—see **Glossary** at the back of this book). Spray the solution on and buff it dry with a soft clean absorbent cloth (paper towels won't hold up long enough for me) or a dry microfiber cloth. If you do leave a streak, it probably won't be as noticeable on small panes, as it would be on a big window. This solution can also be used to clean and debug the sills nicely before you start on the windows.

If the windows aren't too dirty, a barely damp microfiber cloth alone will clean them to a streak-and lint-free finish.

43

What Cuts Cleaning Time the Most?

This is an easy one; there are two biggies. First, dejunk and declutter your place. Junk and clutter are responsible for at least 40 percent of your cleaning efforts. Having too much around makes for much more housework, period. We need to find the floor before we can clean it, and too often, the finding is tougher than the cleaning. Too much furniture, too much paper, too many knickknacks, and too many toys all really slow cleaning. And overstuffed, overdecorated, storage-crammed places even destroy our desire to clean. We can't even hire someone to clean for us because they wouldn't know what to do with all the clutter that's in the way of cleaning. Declutter—it could cut your "housecleaning" in half.

Second, do it now! **"Now" is the magic word in housework.** Any cleaning that should have been done Monday but was put off till Saturday morning ("the big warrior cleaning day") will probably:

- Take twice as much time and effort to do (because stains have set, messes have been spread and scattered, spills and deposits have hardened, etc.)
- Take twice the amount of cleaning chemicals and supplies
- Take twice as much electricity and other energy to do
- Cause more wear and damage to the surface or the item being cleaned

Some people won't wash dishes until they're down to using the decorative ones on the wall! When they finally get around to it, there are two sinks, a whole counter, and a tabletop full of icky, hard-to-clean stuff. This is one reason so many people dread cleaning. They wait till later to do it, or to pick things up and put them back, and it takes forever. Much better to do it now, as you go along, in just minutes or seconds at a time.

My House Needs a Complete Cleaning. Where Do I Start?

Start on the areas that go the fastest! Progress is always encouraging (and besides, you might get ammonia fatigue and someone else will have to finish what's left).

Never start on a bathroom or kitchen—they always look the easiest but take the longest, and if cleaned first always get dirty in the process of cleaning other rooms. My crews were always slower when we started on kitchens, bathrooms, or trash-laden cubbyholes. Their dirt-killing instinct

was dampened and their energy drained for the remaining work. Living rooms, halls, and family rooms are generally the fastest, most motivating areas to commence housecleaning in because they are generally less cluttered and furniture-filled and less dirty. They go fast, and because they seem to be a big part of the job, cleaners feel they are on the way to being done, so they really hustle on the remaining rooms.

✔ As for order within a room, clean ceilings, walls, and woodwork first, and windows, furniture, sinks, floors, and rugs last.

Ah . . . but before you start anything, I'd rustle some help (after draining the swimming pool, hiding the remote, shutting down the computer, and taking the car keys).

How Do I Clean Brick?

This question, like many I get about inside masonry surfaces, is referring to bare or "raw" brick. Because the majority of brick surfaces are left untreated or unsealed, they can easily be penetrated by dirt and stains. Although masonry surfaces are low maintenance, you generally have a rough time getting them clean when they do need it.

To begin with, because brick is so rugged-looking, we often abuse it, and then its homely look prompts us to let it go longer than usual before trying to clean it. When we finally face the job, the brick has had years of attack from stains, fire, smoke, insect sprays, cellophane tape—you name it.

What to clean it with? You may have heard about muriatic acid, because that's what professional bricklayers clean up with after a job. **Don't use it—muriatic acid isn't a cleaner**; bricklayers use it to "wash" a brick surface after building it, because the acid dissolves the binders in the drops of mortar that may have spilled on brick during construction. *Your* brick is embellished with mustard, flyspecks, fireplace smoke, hand oils, dust, glue, cooking oils, drink spills, etc.—muriatic acid won't help with most of those! And, if overused, muriatic acid can weaken mortar and cause structural damage.

Step 1. Brush and vacuum the entire brick surface carefully to pull off and out every bit of dust, loose dirt, or sand.

Step 2. Dry-sponge it (see **Glossary** at the back of this book).

Now you need to make a critical decision. Every brick/stone masonry wall is different in what it's made of and the resulting texture and hardness. If you have a hard, nonporous surface to work with, you can use a heavy-duty cleaner or degreaser solution and scrub brush. If you wet the wall down well, let the solution sit on there for ten or fifteen minutes, and then scrub like a demon, the dirt and crud will roll off in soapy waves. (Be sure to set rolled-up towels at the bottom of the wall first to catch the runoff.)

But if your brick/mortar is soft and porous, the solution might help drive the dinge permanently into the surface and you'll have a still-dirty wall with the wet look. That's why it's important to get as much of the loose dirt off as possible before you use any liquid that might "set" the dirt into the brick or

mortar. If the brick wall is hard, the dirt will float out—then you can absorb it with towels and scrub some more. When the cleaning water starts looking dirty, rinse with clear water and let it run off. I've also cleaned many brick walls with just a dry sponge: Both methods work well.

✔ If you come across a stubborn mark or stain in your cleaning, try paint thinner, a wire brush, or sandpaper on it.

Fireplaces or brick walls that seem to be beyond help can always be sandblasted. Sandblasting does a good job of cleaning but later you'll find sand in everything—your breakfast cereal, clothes, makeup—*everything*. Have sandblasting done by a pro and be aware that the surface will be more porous afterward.

The easiest way to maintain masonry is to apply a coat or two of satin (low sheen) masonry seal *before* a brick or stone wall gets dirty, or right after it's been cleaned and restored. Your wall will then present a surface that discourages dirt and is faster and easier to clean. Ask a reputable masonry dealer what low-sheen finish to use, and also ask about any special soft/porous stone or brick problem you are faced with. I always paint or stain my mortar joints after the wall is in place. It's easy to do and looks ten times as good as most drab concrete mortars—or attempts to mix color *into* the mortar.

On any brick or stone surface, whether you're planning to clean, paint, sandblast, or seal, try a small inconspicuous area first if you have any doubts.

46 ?? ? ? ?

What Is a Wet/Dry Vacuum?
Do I Need One?

Do you need a dishwasher? The same is true of a wet/dry vacuum—if you have it, you'll use it to save you time and depreciation on the house. **A wet/dry is exactly what its name implies: a vacuum that is capable of picking up both wet and dry material.** Wet/dry vacuums are everyday professional tools that have now joined the home cleaner's arsenal. They are practical to own and easy to use in the home, and range in cost from less than $50 (for a local discount store brand) to $475. I'd recommend nothing larger than a ten-gallon capacity with a stainless or plastic tank. (Nonstainless metal tanks are okay, but you have to clean them after each wet pickup so they won't rust.)

A wet/dry vacuum sucks up water or other liquid until the tank is full, at which point a float (which is like a rubber ball) will shut off the air pull (suction) and you'll know it's time to dump the tank, in the toilet or yard. For dry pickup, it uses a simple cloth or paper filter.

You probably already know all the dry jobs you can use a vacuum for, but how about some of these *wet* jobs?

1. Picking up floor-scrubbing water (especially out of those cracks and pits in your floor).

2. Cleaning up food and drink spills before they dry and stain.

3. Picking up vomit, potty spills, pet piddle. (Don't gasp—this is a common and very real cleaning problem.) A wet/dry is a quick, sanitary way to do this. The surface can then be cleaned and rinsed and the water vacuumed away, leaving things fresh, clean, and odor-free.

4. Picking up sink, tub, and rain floods and overflows inside and outside the house.

5. Emptying (from the top) plugged sinks and toilets, or aquariums (once the fish are out, of course!).

The most important wet/dry attachments to own are a brush hand tool, an upholstery tool, and a rubber-tipped squeegee floor tool. If you have some high dust-collecting areas—such as exposed beams—you can get an extra extension hose. The directions that come with the machine will educate you in minutes about the simple maintenance needs of the unit.

What Is the Fastest, Easiest Way to Clean Screens?

Over time, screens become embedded with dust, dirt, bugs, tree sap, bird droppings, and other debris. To clean them:

Step 1

Always take screens down—cleaning them in place is ineffective and often damages them.

Step 2

Lay the screens on a flat, smooth, stable surface covered with an old quilt or blanket so the pressure of cleaning and handling won't stretch or bulge the screen or pull the edge fasteners loose.

Step 3

Mix up some good, strong heavy-duty cleaner or ammonia solution in a bucket and scrub the screens on both sides with a soft-bristled brush.

Step 4

Rinse all the soap and loose dirt out with a hose, shake the worst of the water off, and reinstall.

✔ Any of you brittle-boned creatures over forty (like me)–remember that when you're taking down and putting up the screens, you have both hands off the ladder, so be CAREFUL!

What about Bathroom Carpet?

It stinks! Don't put it in. If it's already installed, pray that your toilet never floods over. **The chances are 100 percent that a bathroom carpet will receive moisture regularly.** When you step out of the tub or shower you drip; the shower splashes over, around, or under the curtain; and the boys have bad aim when they are in a hurry or in the dark. Hair spray and other hair products settle in (and "super hold") it. And every toilet floods over occasionally.

Carpet that gets wet regularly is stiff, it fades, it's ugly, and it smells musty because it houses bacteria. It rots. It is a haven for mildew and bug growth. The next time you stay in a luxury hotel, motel, or condo with bathroom carpet, get down on your knees and sniff—you won't even want to walk on it.

✔ Bathroom carpet takes more time to care for than hard-surface flooring and will require more mainte-nance in the long run.

It looks and feels great when new, but it's only new for the first few days—then it's downhill all the way.

If your bathroom carpet is presently in need of a restorative cleaning job, be sure to use a disinfectant cleaner in your sham-pooing solution, and extract all the moisture you possibly can after rinsing.

How Much Time Do People Spend Cleaning?

Ever since I began my professional housecleaning career in 1954 (at age eighteen) I've been asked this question, and ever since then I've been collecting information right from the source. For more than a quarter of a century now, I've taught audiences all over the United States and have asked them to fill out a comment card telling me, among other things, how long they clean. I haven't compiled or computed all the feedback yet, but I analyzed a good geographical cross section—several thousand cards from around the country—and found the following:

● My informants made no distinctions, drew no lines—cooking, dishes, errands, home maintenance, floors, lawns, and the thousand other details—all of these fell under "housework."

● Aside from the discouraged who answered "more than forty hours" or "not enough" and the many who write, "too much," the calculations seemed to say **the average person spends between two and four hours a day on housework—for all housework and maintenance, not just cleaning.** (Remember this is an *average* that includes everything from single-person households to families with fourteen kids.)

● Many moaned about their workload because of a big house. (I also collected information on the square footage of the average house and found that one-third of the people responding didn't know how big their houses were—a surprise to me as a builder.) **House size alone is deceptive, because a small, compact, densely furnished and decorated home can take more time to clean than a home three times its size.** The age of a home influences how much time is spent **(see page 67, question 28)**, but the amount of clutter in and the number and ages of the people using a home are the biggest factors determining time spent cleaning.

One of my discoveries (no surprise to the women) is that the single biggest problem of housework is: At least 80 percent of the mess in the average home comes from husbands and children, and at least 80 percent of the cleaning up is done by women! That's wrong and it's still a reality today.

Remember that you aren't trying to win any competition. What really matters is how happy you are, and the quality of your relationship with the other members of your household—not how many hours you spend cleaning or how well you clean your house. Don't let the speed (or slowness) of other home cleaners bother you—unless you are a born competitor, and then I suggest you whip through cleaning your own house, start your own business, and capitalize on your accomplishments by becoming the fastest professional cleaner in the world.

50

Is It Cheaper and Better to Make My Own Cleaning Products?

o! It's a joke! All those witches' brews and cleaning concoction recipes you find in books and magazines are desperate "fillers" of odd bits of space and that's about all they're good for. I'll bet there's not one in a hundred of those folks who merrily recommend that you use dried peach fuzz, ground bacon rind, dried bread crumbs, linseed oil, a teaspoon of vinegar, and such who actually use these concoctions themselves. They all go to the supermarket or other supply source like everybody else and buy cleaners that are cheaper, better, safer, and easier to use.

✔ We don't dig our own worms for fishing anymore, cut our own hair, or always mow our own lawns, so why should you feel obliged to blend beeswax and barley into homemade furniture polish? I guess it's a carryover of the pioneer tradition: We feel we're failing somehow if we don't provide some of our own domestic needs.

But commercially manufactured cleaning chemicals, polishes, waxes, and other supplies are safer, more convenient, and much cheaper in the long run. Making your own cleaners requires gathering (often expensive) ingredients and additives, and then containers to mix and store them in. You not only take up your time, but you also run a big risk by making chemical combinations that might be physically harmful.

It isn't worth it. **Buy concentrated cleaners from a janitorial-supply house and mix with water in a spray bottle**—that will satisfy any yearnings for having a hand in making your own "home brew."

If you want to make life simpler, I'd advise you to have only four types of cleaners:

1. An *all-purpose cleaner*. Ideally, this would be a "neutral" cleaner, which means a cleaner that's right in the middle between the 0–7 pH of acids and the 7–14 pH of alkalis. This is gentle and safe to use on most surfaces.

2. A *disinfectant cleaner.* This is for bathrooms and other areas that need germ and odor control. Check the label—"quaternary" is the kind you want.

3. A *quick-evaporating, alcohol-based glass cleaner.* Use this for little windows; squeegee the big ones. This is also great for polishing chrome and other "bright work" in the house.

4. A *heavy-duty cleaner/degreaser.* This is a high-pH cleaner that will dissolve grease and heavy-duty dirt fast.

Buy all of these in concentrate form at a janitorial-supply store **(see page 166, question 73)**, either in jugs or in premeasured packets. Buy 4 one-quart trigger spray bottles and use your own water and the *right* amount of concentrate (not "a little extra to be sure it works good"). If you buy from a reputable place, the cleaner will be as good as or even better than the supermarket variety and much cheaper.

✔ By buying concentrates, you can bring a 6-month supply of cleaners home in a small tote bag. A great percentage of the cleaner you carry out of the supermarket is water; it costs plenty to package, ship, and store water.

When you come up against the question "What cleaner is best?" remember that products and compounds are not magic, but only your tools for the application of intelligent cleaning techniques.

51

Don, If You Had to Choose Between Wallpaper, Wall Covering, and Paint, Which Would You Pick?

Two to one I would paint; however, I might be prejudiced because I'm a professional painter and find application and maintenance of paint pretty simple. I would eliminate wallpaper entirely and stick to vinyl wall covering. Installation is the biggest cost when you cover a wall, so why put on paper that will mark, tear, and stain easily, yet be difficult to clean?

If I were an expert paperhanger, and knew all the ins and outs of handling weaves, foils, and flocks, I might like wall covering as much as I do paint. When I *do* use wall coverings, I use easily maintainable, smooth-surface material. Damage is sure to come to every wall in the form of stains, scuffs, and gouges, so select a wall covering that can be cleaned and repaired easily.

The condition of your walls and your decorating taste are the real factors in the choice. Pitted, cracked, and uneven walls, even with a good paint job, still look cheap and unattractive, plus it generally takes double the effort to paint such a wall.

Wall covering can make a room brighter, warmer, more inviting, even more luxurious. Good-quality vinyl wall covering can also serve a practical function as a wall finish. A patterned wall covering instantly hides defects and upgrades the appearance not only of the wall, but the space. With their vinyl surfaces and tough fabric backings, wall coverings put a good cleanable finish over many surfaces. On wallboard, Sheetrock, and plywood, they minimize joints, cracks, and nail pops. On plaster, they can bridge rough spots and cracks and add a little structural reinforcement. They also offer long-term performance. They're durable, resistant to fading and abrasion, and easy to maintain.

While the initial investment for wall covering is greater, its life is generally more than double that of paint. You usually have to repaint every three years or so, while the normal life of vinyl wall covering is nine or ten years, depending on how you use the house.

Wall covering comes in different grades, and I can only advise, "It costs a dollar less to go first class." High-quality covering can usually be more easily installed, lasts longer, and, of course—the important part—it's easier to clean.

If you choose to paint, use a low-gloss satin enamel. And in painting as in wall coverings, go for the best! The more expensive paint will eventually save you time and money.

52

Is There Any Such Thing as a "Clean" Color?

White, of course, is psychologically "clean." It's become synonymous with purity; hence, we assume "the whiter, the cleaner." Even though white uniforms, walls, furniture, rugs, and vehicles get dirtier faster, because white doesn't hide or disguise dirt or soil, people trust it.

Whites (off-whites) look great in house interiors (walls are one of the most noticeable parts of a home), and can be easily touched up or patched if nail holes or gouges need repairing. Many a handsome home uses off-whites for walls and woodwork and lets drapes, carpet, and furniture (rather than colored walls) add the color.

Yellow is a tough color to "cover" well with when painting walls, and the hardest to make look good when you're cleaning upholstery or rugs. Yellow broadcasts any darker color against it (that's why so many signs and book covers use yellow backgrounds)—and this includes marks or dirt. It's a cheerful color, but when interrupted (which dirt and marks tend to do), you unconsciously dislike it. Yellow and gold carpets are the toughest of all to keep looking good after use, even after cleaning. Blue is another color that's difficult to keep looking good, probably because blues are quiet and restful, so dirt and marks seem more of an intrusion.

Browns and beiges are thought of as earthy or natural colors; hence, dirt and cobwebs, nicks, marks, and handprints won't grate on your nerves as much as they would on light golds or blues. In general, pastels and light shades of any color are hard to maintain, as are extremely dark colors and black (these even show light dust!). Solid colors show more dirt than patterns and textures. If you're *really* interested in hiding dirt, use mid-range tweeds with deep textures on everything you can.

53

Is There a Smart Approach to Bed Making?

Yes! Minimize the number of blankets and covers you use—a couple of thick ones are better than four thin ones that you'll spend the morning smoothing and straightening out. (Be sure the comforter has a cover that zips off for easy laundering, or get one for it.) Don't have excess or overly decorated pillows

or dust ruffles for "fanciness"—they end up being a pain in the neck!

✔ If there are several different sizes of beds in the house (king, queen, double, twin), have different colored linens for each one to save struggling with the wrong sheets on the wrong bed.

Learn how to make a bed so that you only walk around it once; the hotel professionals do it that way. Spread all the covers from one side, then circle around, tucking as you go.

54 ? ? ? ? ?

What Do I Do about My Garage? (After My Big Garage Sale)

It doesn't cost much (in fact it costs less) to have things neat and clean. For example, three 8-foot 2x12s and a few cinder blocks can offer order, safety, and convenience in the form of instant garage storage shelves. Go into your garage and look around. Here are a few ideas that will help you:

1. Store anything light by hanging it as high as possible (but keep it within reach). This takes it out of the "stumbling over" path.

2. Find, buy, or make a wall cabinet (six feet tall if possible) to store small hand tools, paint, lawn and garden supplies, and the like. Concealing stuff that must be stored in the garage has emotional as well as physical advantages.

3. If you wish to mount or hang frequently used hand tools (or display them for friends), the smart, practical, and economical way is to install a 4' x 8' piece of quarter-inch pegboard on the wall (just like you see in store displays)—you can do it easily and a variety of peg hardware is available.

4. Make sure you can see! Most garages are inadequately lighted, which makes them feel like a mineshaft instead of part of a home. The wiring is usually adequate; just convert the incandescent fixtures into fluorescent tube

lights. It will make the garage look better and be safer and cheaper.

5. Paint the garage walls—most garages are unfinished, and thus look naked and shabby. If the walls are bare studs, put up sheet rock and then paint it. Two coats of a good enamel (new or left over from another job) can be applied for a few dollars and will reward you for years.

6. **Prepare and seal the floor, if it's concrete.** This will make it fast and easy to maintain and improve the look and feel of the garage.

- To seal your garage floor, remove all possible furniture, tools, etc., from the floor; sweep up all the surface dirt. Mop on a solution of heavy-duty cleaner, or better yet, light etching acid diluted in water. (Your janitorial-supply or paint store has these—with detailed directions on the label.) Let it soak for a while; if the floor is old and marked, you can then scrub it with a floor machine.

- Flush the solution off now—preferably using a floor squeegee—and rinse with a hose.
- Allow the floor to get good and dry, and then apply transparent concrete seal or an all-purpose seal, either of which can be obtained at a paint or janitorial-supply store. Apply the seal—according to directions—with an applicator that will distribute it in a nice, thin, even coat, and let it dry. I'd advise a second coat to ensure good coverage and that any rough spots are filled.

There's no reason to have a garage that embarrasses or depresses you. With a little planning and work, it can look like the part of your *home* that it is.

55

How Often Should You Clean Drapes?

Why am I asked this question so often? It's like asking, "How often should I take a bath?" It all depends on:

1. The kind of drapes you have (fiberglass, lined, sheer, pleated, etc.). Nylon, for instance, doesn't get dirty as quickly as cotton, and textured drapes don't show dirt.
2. Where they are (a heavy-use area, a study, area where food is prepared or served, etc.).
3. The amount of use and abuse they get (number of kids/cats climbing on them).
4. The professional cleaning facilities available (and their cost).
5. How the drapes look now.
6. How difficult they are to rehang (and who has to hang them).

The average drape-cleaning span in a home is every other year, depending on how dusty your neighborhood is and the heating/ventilating system you have. If they're old, inexpensive drapes, I'd let them go past tolerable, then replace them. If the abuse level (sun, moisture, kids, animals) is high and the drapes are of good quality, I'd probably clean them every year. Make a visual check, and when they're soiled and stained, clean them. Remember, however, that one of the drawbacks of drapes is that they always fade—and fading won't be fixed by cleaning.

When you select your window coverings, remember the window area is a target for activity. The light draws bugs, kids, pets, and people and the convection currents here draw airborne soil. Tinted or smoked glass, vertical blinds, decorative screens, and other alternative window coverings might be worth considering. When you buy and install drapes and curtains, go simple—choose styles and materials that are easy and economical to maintain.

56

What Is the Cleanest Heat?

Fuel-less heating sources such as the sun, and geothermal heating—you can't beat them. After those two, there isn't a big difference between electric, gas, hot water, oil, and coal heat.

The prime reason for dirty homes in the old coal- and wood-burning days was poor insulation and weather stripping. Homeowners who put clean electric heat in an old home without reinsulating found, to their surprise, that their walls got almost as dirty as in the coal days. And those now burning wood (or coal) in newer, well-insulated houses don't have dirty walls. Because of the temperature differential, poorly insulated outside walls pull filth to the inside walls. The wood itself in wood heating systems will create a need for clean-up, as can leaky seams in a woodstove pipe.

Radiant or convection ("still" heat) is a bit cleaner than forced-air heat (whether oil, electric, or gas)—the movement of the circulating air can push around the dirt already present in a house or room. If there is dust in the heating system vents, a forced-air system can push it out into the house. Of course, we all know that good, clean furnace filters make a real difference.

In these days of sealed combustion, high-quality filters, and emission controls, any modern heating method that is functioning properly should not create much dirt either inside or out. But if you have an oil furnace, that is not burning properly (cleanly), you may end up with some soot on the walls.

I'd advise you to **insulate well, select the heat that's most economically sound for your area and life-style, and make sure you perform any necessary maintenance on your heating system**—you'll notice little, if any, difference in the dirt level. Before you blame greasy walls or inside window films on your furnace, check your *cooking venting system*—the problem is probably more the hamburger than the heat source.

What Do You Think of "Lemon Oil" Polishes/Cleaners for Wood?

First off . . . "lemon oil" is not really a cleaner! And it may surprise you to know that it usually has nothing to do with lemons. Most lemon oil is made from high-grade paraffin oil; then lemon scent is added for fragrance. The same is true of the aerosol lemon-scented silicone wood polishes (the TV wonders!)—the lemon smell is just to sell you. Properly used, lemon oil will remove some accumulated grime on wood and can be of some help in maintaining it.

✔ Lemon oil is a penetrant like most oil; it will soak in, condition, and even harden bare wood. This not only helps moisten the wood so it won't dry out, it helps protect it from dampness and stains.

Lemon oil doesn't really have much value on sealed (varnished, painted, or polyurethane-coated) wood surfaces because it can't pass or be absorbed through the coatings and tends to dry slowly and remain tacky, catching dust. On old varnished furniture, however, it may serve a purpose, because even if the finish appears shiny, it often has invisible cracks that allow the oil to seep in and help condition the wood. Lemon oil may also help restore the gloss and depth of a finish if it has worn down over time. If overused, it will build up just like the aerosol gunk spray polishes (top woodworkers basically say polishes should be removed each time before applying more).

If you have a finish that must be "fed," such as natural unfinished wood, lemon oil is good for the purpose (as long as the wood in question isn't in *culinary* use, in which case you must use mineral oil or vegetable oil). It's better to avoid furniture that requires constant oiling and "feeding" or constant polishing. Feeding a family takes enough time and money.

For wooden kitchen cabinets, skip the lemon oil; use a grease-dissolving detergent solution.

How Should I Clean Household Garbage Cans?

Garbage cans get dirty—consider what we put in them!—and need to be cleaned regularly, or they'll get sticky and stinky. About once a month or so, after emptying the cans, take your trusty spray bottle, squirt a heavy mist of disinfectant cleaner solution on them (inside and out), let them sit for a while, then wipe them all over quickly with a white nylon scrub sponge, and rinse them. If tenacious deposits persist, use a nylon scrub brush, or let the pail soak for a while with some all-purpose cleaner in it. If you're in a hurry, turn your containers over a sprinkler head—a vigorous water spray like this can get them pretty clean.

> ✔ For outdoor cans, you can also use a pressure washer. It will get them super clean, and you can use it on the garbage cage area, too, if any. (Sweep first, of course!)

How often a pail should be cleaned depends on the size of your household and the area it is used in. For example, a bathroom container, which has to contend with used dental floss, smeary makeup-remover wipes, etc., needs frequent cleaning. And the kitchen can—filled with dripping cartons, apple cores, and uneaten scrambled eggs—needs routine attention!

I'm not wild about garbage can liners (except for the kitchen), because they're expensive, unsightly, take up storage space, and burden the environment. But liners *do* make can cleaning easier, if you like using them well enough to pay for them. **Lining small garbage cans is an excellent use for those plastic grocery bags** we all accumulate an amazing number of and rarely get around to taking back in to the store's recycling bin.

Remember that most odor comes from bacteria, so if you have a smelly can, some foul thing is probably lodged in there or been leaked in there. Once the can is clean, it will seldom need any deodorizing. If you have a can that seems to have absorbed some bad odors over time (plastic, especially, can do this), treat it with a spray bottle of bacteria/enzyme digester.

What Are the Best Clothes to Wear When Cleaning?

That's a good question—clothes do make a difference. Whites are good for one reason: Your accomplishment is magnified because any dirt shows and looks like progress. That's why professional painters and cleaners wear "whites."

Sneakers or other rubber-bottomed shoes are great for climbing around, traction on ladders, and so forth. Shocks from plugs, appliances, or fixtures are also less likely with rubber or vinyl shoes. Shoes with ties are safer than sandals, which expose your toes and catch on things. And high-heeled shoes, in case there was any doubt in your mind, are *out*!

If you have allergies or sensitive skin (or are working with strong cleaners or corrosive materials), use rubber gloves. But otherwise, it isn't worth having sweaty robot fingers.

Remove jewelry, and tie up your hair if it's long and will get in the way. If your glasses fall off easily, hold them on with an elastic fastener around the back. If you'll be working with strong chemicals that may splash, or if you're cleaning above your head with a lot of debris dropping down, consider safety glasses.

Loose, unbinding, thick but light clothes are best! Don't wear clothes that hang down or bag so much that they catch on ladders or corners or other projections. Wear long pants or jeans, not shorts. Bare arms are okay; bare legs get pinched on ladders or while kneeling. Long sleeves and shirts left out, not tucked in, keep dirt and falling debris off your body. **Wear something you're not afraid to ruin.**

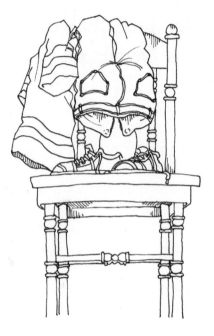

You don't want to dress up to clean, because it'll just waste time and cramp your style, but don't go all the way to Slobsville, either. You might want to keep a little touch of flair in your outfit, because feeling good about yourself helps everything, even cleaning!

60

Don, What Are Some New Cleaning Items That Could Really Make a Difference Around My House?

Since the first edition of this book came out, some fantastic new cleaning tools have appeared on the "Clean Scene." They have revolutionized the way we clean.

Use It Everywhere

The microfiber cleaning cloth works wonders on every surface using plain water or with a cleaner. Made of micro-thin fiber—1/100 the width of a human hair—it can be used to clean a variety of soils off hard surfaces. **Microfiber can even deal with greasy messes and pull spills out of carpet.** Used dry, microfiber has electrostatic properties that help trap and hold dust and dirt so you can dispose of it.

The size and shape of the microfibers, when woven or knitted together, allow them to work so well. Because each strand is smaller than the dirt you are picking up, the fibers fit under and beneath the dirt and soil to clean.

Microfiber cloths are washable and reusable and quality microfiber can be machine-washed up to 300 times—that sure beats using torn-up T-shirts for cleaning! Beware of inexpensive microfiber, however; it leaves lint and will not polish to a streak-free finish.

Microfiber mops are also available, and they clean floors quickly and hold up to seven times their weight in dirt and grime. Wet, a microfiber mop will clean with water alone. Dry, it is unequalled for picking up dust and lint. Microfiber mop-heads, too, can be washed over and over.

Vacuum Like a Pro

I've always used and recommended professional upright vacuums and now there is a model—the Windsor XP12—that solves a lot of problems I've seen in vacuums over the years.

We often turn the height adjustment on our vacuum down so low, for instance, that there is little airflow passing through the carpet—that's no good because the airflow is what creates the suction! The Windsor senses the height of the carpet and automatically adjusts between plush and low pile (or no pile at all), and it adjusts itself when moving from carpet to hard surface floors.

Ever snag a corner of a rug or a blind cord and then hear that munching groan as your vacuum grinds to a halt and then you smell a burning smell? The Windsor automatically shuts off when you wrap something around the beater brush, so it doesn't burn up the belt. It also alerts you when there's a clog or when the bag is full.

This vacuum also eliminates the need to bend over, a godsend for many folks. You can change the bag while standing up or can grab the onboard wand and extend it to reach the baseboards—all without bending over. The suction is great, the machine is light, and best of all . . . sssh . . . it's quiet.

A Cleaning Assistant

As a professional cleaner, I've always noticed how people are fascinated by cleaning carts—such as the maid carts you pass in hotels—that hold all those professional tools and cleaners. Now

Work   Home

there's a cart you can use at home—the Klean-GuRoo cleaning cart. At last, a cart designed to hold the same professional stuff and give you "clean-as-you-go efficiency" to cut home cleaning time in half. **Nothing wastes more time than gathering up supplies and tools every time you want to clean.** The Klean-GuRoo is a home cleaning center on wheels that follows you all through the house. It has shelves and slots to hold towels and mops, brooms and spray bottles, plus all of your cleaning chemicals and, of course, a trash can. You'll never have to rummage under your sink again.

Save Your Back

One of my favorite tools, the angle broom with nylon split-tip bristles, is available in an even more effective design—it now comes with an angled handle to save your back. This new design allows you to reach into corners and under cabinets with ease. **The split bristles act like a zillion tiny brooms to pick up even the finest dirt** and reach the tiny indentations and seams in many types of floors.

Snip and Go

Premeasured cleaners such as those from PortionPac have been around for years, yet they remain a great convenience and savings many people aren't aware of. You just snip one of these little plastic envelopes open, pour it in a quart spray bottle, and fill with water.

Premeasured cleaners are easy to use and assure that your cleaning solutions are never over- or under-diluted. Best of all, they're inexpensive—less than half what you pay for jugs of cleaner at the supermarket! You can find them at janitorial-supply stores and from the Cleaning Center.

What Do I Do about Hard Water Spots on My Windows?

irst, eliminate the culprit (sprinkler, hose, or whatever) that's causing the problem. Don't blame it on rain—rainwater is soft and doesn't leave mineral deposits.

A mild acid cleaner will dissolve most mineral deposits on outside glass. Janitorial-supply stores will have one or more products of this type under various names and weaker solutions are available at supermarkets. I use Showers-n-Stuff and a non-abrasive white nylon scrub pad or hourglass scrubber (see **Glossary** at the back of this book) to speed up the work. Don't use colored scrub pads, steel wool, or sponges with colored nylon pads attached, as they have abrasives in them that can scratch glass. Also, don't use strong acid cleaners such as toilet bowl cleaners or drain cleaners. They can damage metal, brick, paint, and hands.

The minerals on the windowpane build up over time and often must be removed the same way—one layer at a time. So, if spots remain, reapply the cleaner and let it sit on there for up to five minutes before scrubbing and rinsing. Mild acid cleaners are also safe to use for deliming bathroom sinks, chrome fixtures, and tub and shower units.

After removing the deposits, clean the window with your squeegee. Long-standing hard water deposits may have fused with the surface and become unremovable.

For the toughest hard water spots and ugly haze, there is a very strong commercial-grade paste that must be used with caution. It's called Once-Over. Write to me at P.O. Box 700-DV, Pocatello, ID 83204, for information about ordering it.

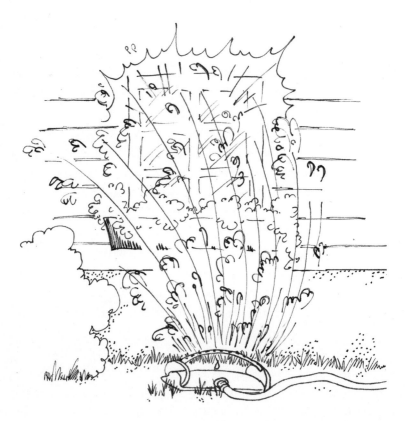

How Do You Clean Carpeted Stairs and Carpet Edges?

The bad news is that carpet edges—the one or two inches next to the baseboard or stairs that the vacuum never seems to get—are one of the most telltale signs of poor housekeeping. A trained eye will pick it up two seconds through your front door. Because edges are not exposed to traffic (which means no physical damage to the carpet) the problem is mostly visual. **Vacuum the edge with your vacuum attachments every so often (or whenever you're feeling really ambitious).** The rest of the time, sweep any visible cobwebs, dirt, or dust away from the base- or mopboards with a broom or damp towel, and then do your regular vacuuming.

Treat stairs the same way as regular carpet edges. The back and side edges of stair carpets receive little or no traffic so dirt doesn't damage them. The step—especially the center two feet—gets 90 percent of the abuse, and it is heavy! Once a month or so, get someone to hold the vacuum and quickly take a small nozzle (to concentrate the suction) and vacuum the edge. Or you can take a damp towel, get on your hands and knees, and in about five minutes whip down the stairs removing the "fur" and dust from the edges.

For the center of the stair, use your beater upright or canister vacuum. If it's too heavy to use on the stairs once a week,

I'd say it's too heavy to use anywhere in the house. You can purchase a nice professional Windsor upright vacuum that will do a super job on all routine household vacuuming.

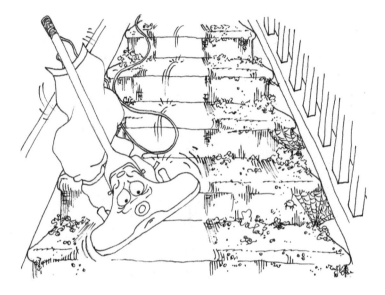

P.S. Black deposits around the edges of carpeting may have nothing to do with how often you clean the edges. It may be carbon deposited by the heating and air circulation systems in your home. This kind of discoloration is very hard to remove. So, if it doesn't vacuum up and spotters don't remove it, call in the pros.

63 ? ? ? ? ?

The Grout in My Bathroom Tile Is Grungy—How Do I Clean It?

The typical grungy shower has a buildup of body oils and soap scum as well as hard water deposits, maybe mildew, too. Clean it with a mild nonphosphoric acid (the base of many tile- and grout-cleaning compounds); the best I've used is Showers-n-Stuff. It cuts through the soap scum and body oils as well as the mineral deposits. It's less dangerous to use than harsh acids and does just as well.

To clean stained and dirty grout, use wax stripper or heavy-duty cleaner and a grout brush (see **Glossary** at the back of this book). Use bleaching cleanser on stubborn spots. Rinse well.

To clean mildewed grout, scrub with a 1:5 solution of liquid chlorine bleach and water, then rinse well.

Dirty mortar joints are a universal problem that can be reduced, if not prevented, by some precautionary measures:

1. Always make sure grout is sealed before you use it, or after a major clean-up, if it's never been sealed. Your tile dealer or local home improvement store can tell you what you will need and show you how to do it. Grout is best sealed when new. Once oils, stains, and moisture have penetrated it, sealing is less effective. Masonry sealer can be applied with

a small brush to the grout seams only. Silicone sealers in spray bottles are also available. Any type of sealer may have to be reapplied periodically.

2. Squeegee or wipe down the shower walls after every use.

3. Clean regularly with a disinfectant cleaner, and in the long run you'll spend less time "grout routing."

4. Make sure that your bathroom is well ventilated, to help reduce mildew.

5. If you're building or remodeling, use darker mortar. It looks nice and eventually will help hide the problem. You can also use mortar with a latex or acrylic admix, which is harder and more stain resistant. Smaller grout joints will also reduce the problem area. Avoid miracle tub and shower mortar whiteners—most of them are just more expensive versions of a household bleach solution.

How Should I Clean My Ceiling Fan?

Super fast, as long as you don't turn it on first! Most of the dirt on a ceiling fan is the same stuff that accumulates on top of the refrigerator. The dust floating around the house joins up with airborne grease and oil, alights on the fan, and sticks—especially to the blades. Then more dust sticks to the gummy film that develops.

Ceiling fan blades are often wood but with several coats of varnish, polyurethane, or other water-resistant finish, so you can use liquid on them. Grease is an acidic kind of soil, so a good alkaline cleaner is what you want to remove it. **A solution of hand dishwashing detergent, or if the grime is really thick, heavy-duty cleaner, is what you want to use.**

Make sure the fan is turned off, then lightly spray or wipe the blades with the solution. Let it sit on there a minute or two, then wipe dry with a thick, thirsty terry cleaning cloth. Any stubborn spots that remain can be scrubbed with a dampened white nylon scrub pad, and then wiped dry. With a good sturdy ladder, spray bottle in one hand and cleaning cloth in the other, you can do this on one climb, hooking the spray bottle in your belt after spraying and using your free hand to hold the fan blades as you clean them (you always want to be careful not to jar fan blades out of balance, or you'll end up with a shaky, noisy fan).

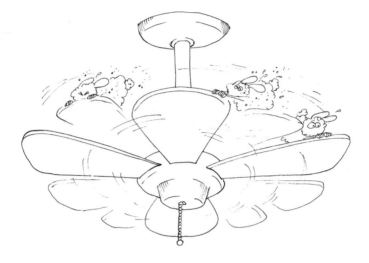

Before you come down, debug, defuzz, and shine the motor housing by spraying a little of your cleaning solution onto the terry towel and wiping the housing clean. Take it easy with the moisture here, as around any electrical device.

Once the fan blades are truly clean, they'll have a slick surface that slows the deposit of new dirt. **The smart approach here is more frequent dusting,** to remove the dust before it has a chance to combine with grease into a stubborn, sticky film, and a long-handled lambswool duster is the perfect tool for the job.

Why Do My Floors Go Dark Under Mats and Appliances?

I t could be the old wax yellowing, chemicals migrating out of low-quality mat backing into the floor, or even the flooring material itself. **Most floor coverings and paints will yellow if kept in the dark for an extended period of time.** The UV rays in normal sunlight (or even artificial light) have a bleaching action and tend to keep white materials white. When kept in the dark, away from this natural whitening action, most flooring materials—even enamel paint—tend to darken and yellow with age. If you've ever removed a picture

from a painted wall and found a permanently darkened area behind it, you know what I'm talking about.

✔ There is no easy cure for this phenomenon, as this type of yellowing has become a part of the paint or flooring itself and cannot be cleaned off.

Many people don't use floor mats for this reason. Personally, I *like* the yellowing under good-quality mats—it forces you to keep the mats in place, resulting in a longer-lasting floor and a cleaner house. The benefits of matting to you, your floors, and the entire house **(see page 97)** far outweigh the risk of slight discoloration "where a mat was"!

How Should I Clean a Telephone?

The telephone has to be running a strong second in the filth finals **(see page 168 for the first place finisher)**! An assortment of dirty (and often oily) ears, hands, mouths, and cheeks are in close germ-spreading communication with a phone every day—so use a disinfectant cleaner solution in a plastic spray bottle when you clean the phone, which should be often. A phone in a home should be cleaned at least monthly, and weekly—not weakly—in a commercial building.

Never spray a phone directly, especially near the transmitter holes on the mouth- and earpieces, or the touch keys, because moisture might cause a malfunction. Spray the solution onto a soft cloth and wipe the phone, then polish with a dry cloth.

✔ Every so often, dampen a soft cloth with all-purpose cleaner and clean the phone cord by running it through your hand—you'll be amazed how dirty it is.

Never use harsh cleaners or abrasives on a phone because phone plastic, like all plastic, can't take it.

How Do I Clean My "Cottage Cheese" Ceiling?

The sprayed-on "cottage cheese"–type ceilings have a rough look, but this is actually a soft, pliable finish, generally made of little beads of Styrofoam, which act not only as a beautifying texture, but also as an acoustical surface. The combination of its rough texture and its soft, absorbent properties makes a cottage cheese ceiling very difficult to clean, even with the handy dry sponge.

When cleaning is necessary, if a dry sponge or vacuum dust brush won't do it (and the ceiling soil is only normal), the oxidizing treatment outlined on **pages 16–18** will do a good job of making it appear cleaner.

You have one last alternative: spraying or rolling on a coat of paint (a real job). First, clean the ceiling as best you can with a sponge dipped in degreaser solution, wiping it on and then wiping it off with a clean, dry cloth; then let it dry. Now, apply latex enamel paint with a deep-pile roller. Two coats may be needed. Painting restores the fresh, clean look of a new ceiling, but it might look a little gobby and detract from the acoustical value.

The liabilities of this type of ceiling finish far outweigh the assets. Thank heaven cottage cheese ceilings have gone out of style.

Is Aluminum Always So . . . Ugly?

Be satisfied with aluminum: It doesn't rust, fade, peel, chip, or rot. It might oxidize a little (that cloudy gray film on the surface), but it stills looks okay without much maintenance. Most aluminum, whether on inside or outside fixtures (especially windows and doors) has a burnished or brushed—not shiny and smooth surface—and is not intended to look spit-polished all the time. And the aluminum windows and doors with tough enamel paint electrostatically applied to the surface (anodized) are a great away around the "dingy aluminum" problem.

But if the oxidation on plain old ordinary aluminum gets intolerable to you, mix up some all-purpose cleaning solution, scrub with a white nylon pad, and then wipe it dry. This won't change the aluminum's appearance much, but there'll be a lot of black marks on your cloth, psychologically creating the impression that the aluminum is *now* clean—and you'll live happily ever after.

Don't use strong cleaners of any kind on aluminum, as they can discolor or pit the surface.

Where Do You Draw the Line Between Clean Enough and Too Clean?

As my grandma (a mother of fifteen children who always had a clean house) said, "If there are dirty dishes in the sink and my husband wants me at that moment to be or go someplace with him (fun or work), that's clean enough!" Or as a woman in Randolph, Utah, wrote on one of my seminar comment cards, "I can tolerate dust till it's ankle-deep, I'd rather rock babies 'cause babies don't keep."

Thousands of chronic cleaners have swept family and friends out the door because they didn't know when clean was clean enough. And an equal number of "grime lovers" have accomplished the same thing with dirt and disorganization.

Somewhere between the health hazard, Bert Buried, and the compulsive cleaner, Annie Septic, is a standard that fits your values, energies, available time, and personal need for cleanliness and order. Decide on the level of cleanliness, order, and sanitation that suits you emotionally, physically, and financially, and hold to it; remember that *you* must be comfortable with the level—double standards never work.

There is "clean" dirt and "dirty" dirt. The piles of sawdust on the floor when the kids are practicing their wood-carving in your basement are clean dirt. There's nothing wrong with *making* a mess—most accomplishment requires a mess of

some kind—the problem is in *leaving* the mess. We clean for three basic reasons:

1. Aesthetics (so things look and feel good)
2. Health (to kill germs and keep things safe)
3. Economy (cleaning cuts depreciation of your home and furnishings)

Decide how much each of these goals means to you, and make yourself a cleaning schedule that reflects this.

70

I Have Deep-Textured Wall Covering— Should I Give Up Trying to Clean It?

You remove dirt and film from any indented or textured surface in two stages:

1. Dissolve
2. Wipe/remove

Too many of us are used to wiping off easy, smooth surfaces and forget that **dissolving and suspending is the number one approach to any cleaning.** Mere wiping just glides over any little pockets full of dirt. If you use the right cleaning solution, the deposit in the grooves will soften and "float" loose so that a thick terry cloth or a mild brushing action will extract it.

Apply a warm solution of all-purpose cleaner to the wall covering; a lather can be worked up on the vinyl using a soft-bristled brush. Give extra attention to loosening dirt from the depressed areas of deeply embossed wall covering, and then removing the suds or soap (rinse thoroughly with clean water). Drying the surface well with a terry towel should absorb any cleaning residue.

Remember, wall coverings generally contain a chemical compound called a "plasticizer." The plasticizer is necessary to condition and soften the vinyl so it can be rolled and applied easily. If dirt is allowed to stay on the surface for a long time, the plasticizer tends to absorb dirt, making the wall covering even more difficult, if not impossible, to clean.

Many stubborn surface stains can be removed with isopropyl alcohol on a hanky-sized cloth. (DO NOT use carbon tetrachloride or lacquer solvents or any abrasive for cleaning vinyl wall coverings.)

71

Does Scotchgard Pay?

It does for the 3M Company! "Scotchgard" is a trade name for a soil retardant used on fabrics and fibers to help them resist dirt and stains. 3M has a soil retardant specifically for carpeting called Carpet Protector. Several companies besides 3M make soil retardants.

Guarding against penetration of soils, liquids, and stains by applying a protective coating generally does pay: Scotchgard

does an excellent job on 95 percent of the upholstery fabric I've used it on or seen it used on. It preserves and protects, making furnishings look better and wear longer. On carpet I'll make that about 75 percent, because people have a tendency to let treated surfaces go, even though dirt still gets on them.

Scotchgard (or other soil retardants, such as my own Time Saver Carpet and Fabric Protector) will pay off if:

1. Carpet, upholstery, or other items are new or cleaned thoroughly prior to application.
2. The fabric's manufacturer okays soil retardant use.
3. The retardant is applied properly. (Follow the directions.)
4. The surfaces are maintained thereafter. Too many people think soil retardant–treated surfaces are self-maintaining—they don't have to be cleaned ever again. This often makes the retardant do more harm than good, because we stop taking care of that surface at all.

And last . . .

5. If you hire a professional to apply retardant, get references.

Most new carpet and much upholstered furniture have soil retardant in the fabric already. If it doesn't, apply some yourself, following the directions carefully, before the item in question is put in use.

Why Do I Get Leaks and Yellow Stains on My Walls in Late Winter and Early Spring, Even Though My Roof Is in Perfect Shape?

The thawing and freezing of early spring causes an ice buildup in the eave and gutter areas of a roof. This buildup often acts like a dam, trapping melt-and-runoff water and causing it to back up under the flashing of shingles or tile roofing. The water leaks through and causes the wood of the roof to swell and rot. It will also deteriorate and stain the wall material itself

(paneling, Sheetrock, or plaster) and damage the paint or wall covering, causing more cleaning and repair work for you.

Take care to keep ice off the eaves. It can be chipped off with a hand tool, but the best way is to put a heat cable in any persistent buildup area (usually the north side). Heat cable (sometimes called heat tape) is a simple electrical wire that looks like a heavy extension cord. It warms up when it's plugged in, and when it's laid in the gutter or buildup areas of the roof, it keeps ice from accumulating.

Many moisture stains on exterior or interior walls (those awful yellow-brown splotches) are from saturated, dissolving Sheetrock and generally can't be removed. A quick paint touchup is the answer, but be sure to undercoat or use a sealer such as KILZ or shellac on the stain first so it won't bleed through.

Where Can I Get Professional Cleaning Supplies and Equipment?

The quality, time-savings, and safety of professional cleaning supplies make it worth the effort to seek them out; they're cheaper in the long run, too, although they may seem more expensive because they're often in concentrated form. Most people live within range of a reputable janitorial-supply house (look in the **Yellow Pages** or **online** right now).

When you go into these stores, feel welcome and don't act like a cow in a circus. Act like the professional that you are! (You've probably done more sink scrubbing than a lot of professional janitors have.) **The staff will help you choose the best tools for the job at hand and give you expert instruction on how to use them,** and they will help you find the professional chemicals in the amount you need. What they don't stock, they can get for you. Most of them buy from a distributor/jobber or direct from a factory outlet at a 40 to 50 percent discount, and on a cash purchase most of them will turn around and give you 20 to 30 percent discount off retail, especially if you get together with a few of your friends or neighbors for buying power! If you live in a small town like I do (McCammon, Idaho—population 806), save up until you get to the big town, then splurge (you should only have to visit the store once a year anyway)!

Read the "Miscellaneous For Sale" newspaper section, or watch for bankruptcy or business close-outs—used professional cleaning equipment is tough to get rid of, so you'll get some good deals. I saw a friend pick up a (dirty but in perfect shape) 13" buffer for $5. I picked up a $600 floor machine and a big $1,200 extractor—$250 for both. Look for the 12" to 13" commercial floor machines for scrubbing floors or bonnetting (surface cleaning) your carpet. Look for a good upright or wet/dry vacuum (preferably the ten-gallon size). The **Glossary** at the back of this book lists some of the professional supplies and equipment most likely to be useful to a homeowner. Buy your chemical cleaners in concentrated form and dilute them yourself. The quality of professional materials will save you tons of money and time.

To order professional tools and supplies by mail, send a postcard with your name and address for a free catalog/newsletter to: The Cleaning Center, P.O. Box 700-DV, Pocatello, ID 83204, or e-mail me at *don@aslett.com.*

What Is the Dirtiest Place in the House?

A question with an undisputed answer: the doorknobs. Many guess "the toilet" or "my kid's room." These might be dirty or messy, but for true "bad dude" dirt, anything handled constantly with our hands wins the prize. Hands scratch rumps, pick noses, get coughed and sneezed into regularly, and handle all kinds of things, and they can and do transfer soil and germs.

Once a month or so hand a spray bottle of disinfectant cleaner to someone (one of the older kids would be perfect) and have him or her clean the following with the "spray and wipe" method: **Spray on some cleaner, let it sit a minute or two, and then wipe it off with a clean, dry terry cleaning cloth.** Here's a checklist:

- ❏ All doorknobs
- ❏ All drawer and cabinet handles
- ❏ All fridge handles
- ❏ All faucet handles
- ❏ All chair backs
- ❏ All broom handles
- ❏ Handles of buckets and baskets
- ❏ All suitcase handles
- ❏ And the spray bottle itself!

When cleaning these next three, spray the cleaner on the cloth, not the item, and use it to wipe the item clean.

- ❑ All phones
- ❑ Knobs on TVs, VCRs, whatever
- ❑ All light switches

Now look at the formerly white terry towel and think of the colds you may have just saved the family—clean is rewarding!

75

How Do You Clean Off Masking Tape and Other Sticky Residue?

First, you pull or gently scrape off what will come off (remember, when it's fresh it all comes off). If it's been on awhile—such as when you tape around a window to stop air leaks or use masking tape to hang a poster—when you try to get it off you'll leave some of the glue and parts of the tape.

De-Solv-it is a popular citrus-based remover that can be used safely on many surfaces, and it's my favorite so far. Acetone, nail polish remover, or lacquer thinner will also remove tape residue,

and these removers won't harm glass, baked enamel (such as on refrigerators), or other nonreactive surfaces, but can harm some paint and plastic surfaces and even take the finish off wooden furniture. Be sure to check the label and to test in an inconspicuous place before you use them on a surface you're not sure of.

✔ To hang posters, drive tiny nails or brads–they never fail and leave only a minute hole when removed.

Don't use masking tape any more than you need to. For painting, a good slant-tip sash brush in most people's hands can cut a finer line than with the tape's help!

76

What about Cleaning Those Small Appliances?

Seems like all of us have an almost embarrassing inventory of small appliances, and most of these are found in the kitchen. Toasters, mixers, blenders, squeezers, can openers, bread machines, coffee and espresso makers, coffee bean grinders, and so on. And even as these are hogging and clogging the counter, we are watching TV and home show demonstrations and lusting for more of these clever food preparation mechanisms.

Many of these have some special cleaning requirements that the little booklet that came with them will detail, but the cleaning and care of small appliances can be lumped into a "general principles" approach.

Anything used with and around food should be cleaned immediately after use. Waiting will double or triple the time and energy required to clean it, and mean more wear on and possible damage to the appliance, not to mention bacteria growth. Small appliances are often dirtier than large ones, because we handle them with our hands, often in a hurry.

These mainly electrical appliances for the most part can't be immersed in or flooded with water. So after unplugging them and removing any loose debris (peelings or crumbs or whatever), wipe all accessible surfaces down well with a sponge or cloth wet with dish detergent solution, or if safe to do so, spray

them with all-purpose cleaner. Let the solution remain on there for a few minutes so the chemical action of the detergent has a chance to dissolve grease and oil and loosen food smears and in general allow you to wipe instead of scrub. Then rinse or wipe-rinse with a cloth moistened in clean water, and polish them dry with a cleaning cloth. If you have let them go and soil is caked on there, wet them down a little more and leave the solution on longer, and scrub with a brush if necessary. Don't forget to clean the base and underneath—it's amazing how soiled the "sitting area" will get.

✔ Do it now . . . don't allow anything to build up or accumulate!

Is It True That You Can Tell a Couple's Relationship by Looking in Their Refrigerator?

How come everyone in the world heard me make that statement? But even things said in jest in TV interviews have meaning, so here goes . . .

I'm a firm believer in a principle called *carryover*. In plainer words, the personal characteristics you exhibit in one situation are essentially the same ones you will show in other, totally unrelated situations. A person who's sloppy in appearance will generally be sloppy in speech, promise keeping, and gardening. If you are an aggressive competitor on the tennis court, you generally will be that way in business meetings, apple picking, and style of dress.

✔ The refrigerator is probably the most personal of all furniture and appliances–behind its door (and often in front of it!) is a composite picture of your organization, judgment, decisions, hopes, failures, and successes. It's not open to the world but you can tell a lot by taking a hard look in it.

Are you the type who lets the refrigerator go and go and go, cramming in more and more and finally going to two-story

stacking, ignoring spills and vegetables that have shriveled beyond identification—then suddenly in a dedicated attack of repentance you whip into it, leaving it gleaming and immaculate? You are probably also letting relationships or living strains and irritations go, go, go, until they are intolerable—then in a big weeping, soul-cleansing trauma, you sweep your cowering family into a confrontation, followed by a tearful "kiss and make up" all-is-well. But then you start stacking the fridge again, putting lids on the problems that you'd rather delay making decisions on. You do this until the fridge (or family situation) stinks and is ready to explode—and then you dive in again and make peace, love, apologies, promises, etc.

Those who keep their refrigerators bare (I mean not a morsel to snack on—not a saucer of cold peaches or a peeled boiled egg in there) often have empty, cold relationships with family and associates.

The person who can't manage to put a lid on a smelly container in the refrigerator probably can't keep the lid on a neighborhood secret.

If you have disguised or hidden "no-nos" (fattening chocolates) stashed in secret places in your fridge, you'll probably have other hidden things (gifts, rash purchases, damaged things, spare money) no one else knows about.

If a fridge is dominated by processed foodstuffs, it generally signifies your time with loved ones is limited.

Before any of you sit back and feel too smug, the same kinds of diagnoses can be made from toolboxes, lockers at school or work, knapsacks, backpacks, briefcases, and so on and so forth.

78

How Do I Care for My Rock or Tile Entryway Floor?

ock, brick, ceramic, "Mexican," quarry, and assorted earth tiles are extremely durable flooring materials and can be kept looking good with a minimum of care. To illustrate my point, I'll ask you to recall the "rock" tile floors in the large shopping malls you've undoubtedly patronized. Did the floor look dull, dry, and scuffed? Probably not. In most malls, the floors are kept clean and glowing to present a positive image to the customers. The owners, expecting thousands of people a day to be walking up and down the broad thoroughfares, choose flooring noted for its durability and ease of maintenance. When you compare the mall's traffic to that in your entryway (thirty or forty per day, maybe) there's no reason your floor can't look bright and shiny all the time.

You can keep rock floors looking "rustic" (like the resort lodge's) or highly polished ("downtown"). Some rock or tile *has* to have a finish applied to its naturally dull or porous surface. The proper finish not only seals and smoothes out the surface, but it also deepens and brings out the natural colors and beauty of the stone or tile. **If you have a problem tile or rock floor, most likely the problem lies in your choice of finish products and their application.** Many people, suffering from the no-wax floor syndrome, make the mistake of putting a varnish-type finish on their floors, and expect it to last forever. The finish looks great for a while, but eventually ends up scabbing and peeling like a sunburned back. The secret lies in putting down a permanent, penetrating sealer, topped with a renewable finish material (to *keep* it looking good).

The sealer can be an easy-to-use water emulsion type or a resinous product, but in any case, it should be a *penetrating* sealer. You want your sealer to penetrate and seal—not leave a thick film on top of the stone. Sealers are very hard and brittle, and if you have a thick layer of sealer on top of your stone, it will tend to chip off and peel just like the varnish does. After proper sealing, apply several coats of a good floor finish to protect the surface and to give the desired smoothness and gloss. This can be a liquid acrylic finish like you use on your vinyl floors, or a paste wax. Waxes and other finishes are softer than the sealer, and thus should not chip or peel. They will *wear* off, though! The finish coat must be renewed from time to time to maintain its beauty, and should not be allowed to wear down to the seal coat. The finish can be stripped off and reapplied without removing the sealer.

After your entry floor is properly finished and looking great, don't forget to put down a good entry mat **(see page 97)** to protect the heavy traffic area just inside the door, and to keep off the grit. These mats are available in nice earth tones and decorator colors to enhance the beauty of your natural stone or tile floor.

How Should I Clean Vinyl Siding?

Vinyl siding is on millions of home exteriors now, and thousands more every day. For durability and freedom from periodic scraping and repainting, it's a great improvement over the old wooden siding. It may not need to be painted, but (as those of us who have it have discovered) it does need to be cleaned.

Vinyl siding gathers dust and dirt from rain and wind and the atmosphere, cobwebs, droppings from birds and insects, and marks from human wear (like barbecue soot, smudges and marks from dirty fingers, tool handles, and even baseballs and dirty snowballs!). Not to mention that moss or monster mildew that often appears on the north side.

✔ The vinyl in vinyl siding is solid, meaning the color isn't just a coating—it runs all the way through. Although that vinyl surface is tough and resistant, keep harsh acids, abrasives, and bleach-type cleaners off it.

You have three relatively easy options for cleaning here, your choice depending on the condition of the siding and your own ambition.

To clean vinyl siding you can:

1. Hose it: Setting the nozzle to get the most concentrated spray out of a plain garden hose will wash off loose dirt and

dust, and won't cause a leak or harm the vinyl, no matter how much you flood it. Hosing will remove some surface dirt, but it won't get the siding truly clean. Embedded dirt, moss, and many bug marks will not come off this way.

2. Pressure wash it: The 1,300 p.s.i. home pressure washing units available now use a minimum of water and will, without the aid of any chemicals, knock off dirt, even mildew, much faster, better, and safer than bleach or any other method of cleaning. Plus the mildew seems to stay off longer after pressure washing. Just follow the instructions that come with it, including all precautions for your own safety and that of the surface you're cleaning.

3. Brush wash: Some house exteriors, due to their location, pollutants in the air, etc., will collect a grimy or oily residue, and any vinyl siding that has been neglected for a while will collect a variety of stubborn marks. Either of these situations calls for a detergent and some scrubbing. Any all-purpose cleaner will do, just dilute it according to directions and then apply with a car-washing type brush on a long handle. Leave the solution on there a minute or two after you apply it, to help emulsify and remove the dirt. Do a small area at a time, working from top to bottom, and be sure to rinse it before the solution has time to dry. The little bit of detergent that washes off won't hurt the flowerbeds or the lawn.

The lower part of the house, easily reached from the ground, will usually be the dirtiest part. For anything higher, a pro extension handle saves lugging ladders and leaning them against the siding (leaving marks).

Remember that everything fades over time in sunlight, so if your siding doesn't look quite as bright as previously, even after cleaning, it may be faded.

P.S. When you come across marks on lower parts of the house use a white nylon-backed sponge dipped in all-purpose cleaner solution to remove them. If you run across a spot of paint, ink, or the like, a bit of paint thinner (mineral spirits) on a terry towel with a determined finger under it should dissolve and remove the mark. Rust comes out with Whink or a mild bathroom acid. Try lacquer thinner (used sparingly) for the really stubborn spots. If all else fails, a dab of matching paint or caulk should take care of it.

How Do I Get Paint and Other Hard Specks Off Windows?

Most likely, those specks are dried paint from either brush lap or drip or paint gun overspray. Ninety percent of window glass is smooth and hard enough to be scraped (but be sure not to try to scrape Plexiglas). The scrape system works great on labels or window decorations you wish to remove, as well as on paint. Always use a new razor blade in a scraper holder—don't use it loose by itself because you'll have less control. **Don't use the plastic windshield scraper you got at the service station**—it's fine for scraping frost, but a car windshield is different from house glass.

Before you start scraping, wet the window with soapy water—this lubricates the razor and helps loosen and release specks from the surface for easy removal. When scraping with the razor blade, *go in only one direction: FORWARD.* Dragging a razor back over the window does nothing to remove anything—but it will trap sand; grit; mortar specks; old, hard paint flakes or whatever under the blade and often scratch or damage the glass.

You can dissolve paint with paint removers, but this is messy and often gets on the sill (where you don't want the paint removed!). But dissolving is about the only way to go on

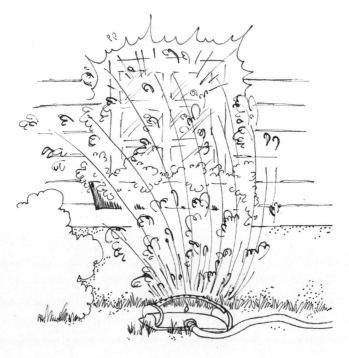

rough-textured windows. Don't leave any drips or streaks of removers on the window; they will harden and be almost as tough to get off as the paint was. Wash and squeegee the window after you finish!

Is There a Painless Way to Clean Louvered Doors?

The most painless is to eliminate them! Many closet doors aren't necessary. They're always open anyway, and even if closed, dust does drift through the louvers.

Louvers may serve a purpose (ventilation) and even be decorative, but they are a high-maintenance item. Louvered doors have scores of horizontal surfaces that invite the settling of dust. Those little slats are so close together, it's hard to get in there where the dust is.

The first approach to take here is a vacuum with a dust brush attachment. You can make quick passes over the louvers, brushing the dust loose and picking it up at the same time. I love Eureka's Mighty Mite for a job like this—a sturdy little 12-amp canister that you can carry around, rather than drag.

The second cure for dusty louvered doors is regular dusting with a lambswool duster or quality feather duster such as Texas Feathers. What these don't pick up, they knock off for a floor vacuuming to dispose of.

Third is a slow but thorough method for built-up dust. Wrap a Masslinn disposable dustcloth (see **Glossary** at the back of this book) around a ruler or paint stirring stick a couple of times. Run this "dusting blade" inside and along the louvers and you'll get all the dust, on both the bottom and the top. When one dustcloth fills up, replace it with a new one. You can use this same basic method to wash louvered doors, when it becomes necessary. Use a spray bottle to shoot all-purpose cleaner solution between the slats. Then wrap a thick terry towel or cleaning cloth around a yardstick or paint stirring stick, insert the stick between the slats, and run it back and forth a few times to loosen and pick up the crud. Keep switching to new areas of the towel as you work your way along.

✔ Good matting (see question 41, page 97), regular vacuuming, and clean furnace filters will cut down the need for tight-space dusting in general.

82

How Do You Clean the Tracks of Shower and Patio Doors, Medicine Cabinets, Etc.?

Any door mounted on a base (bottom) track will someday cause a problem. The wear of rollers and tracks is accelerated by the dirt buildup and water runoff from the windows and doors. Moisture turns the accumulated dirt into a gummy residue that "freezes" or binds up rollers when the residue gets hard.

The solution is simple—clean and maintain tracks regularly. That means don't wait until the doors are beginning to stick. Vacuuming tracks does little good because anything loose is quickly ground into gummy stuff. Take a spray bottle of all-purpose cleaner solution and generously squirt all over and inside the tracks and rollers, and let it sit on there awhile to dissolve the hardened dirt deposits. Then wrap a screwdriver with a soft cloth that has some body to it, like terry cloth, and wipe out the gunk. It's a little awkward, but a couple of passes and the track will clean up. A grout brush also works well here.

If the track is kept clean, the rollers will stay clean and operable.

Don't lubricate tracks with graphite, petroleum jelly, or oil, because this will increase gunk buildup. In general, I advise two things:

1. Get top roller tracks instead of bottom tracks if you have a choice next time—and buy the best you can.
2. Keep them clean.

I've Heard That Men Are Doing More Housework Than They Used To. Is That True?

It's definitely more than it used to be, but it still isn't as much as it should be. I've collected thousands upon thousands of comment cards over the years on which I asked, "How much cleaning is done by spouse and children?" The answers, even in this day of sexual equality and two-career households, are surprising. When I was in London on a book tour once, the BBC did an on-air poll that explained why the "latest study" of how much housework men do never seems to quite jibe with life as we know it on the homefront. A group of British men were asked how much of the housework they did. Most said, "about 50 percent." When the wives of those same men were asked, they doubled over with laughter—5 percent was closer.

✔ It isn't fair, it isn't right—but cleaning as we know it has generally fallen to the woman's lot and even with most women out working in the world, they still haven't been "relieved" of the brunt of home care.

Think a minute. Where did you—or anybody—learn to clean? You can go to school and learn to use a computer, play a horn, dribble a ball, operate on a frog, split an atom, identify historical figures, and 10,000 other edifying, useful things. But where did you learn to clean? From your mother—and she learned from her mother, who learned from her mother, who learned from her mother, who learned from her mother (who even made her own soap and underwear). Way back, it was established that the man hunted, fished, and brought home the food, and the woman gathered wood and cleaned up after all three (wood, food, and man). Along with the tradition of how and what to clean came down *who* should clean (the woman), and people are still being taught—by their mothers.

Everyone in the family participates in big Sunday dinners; tag football; popcorn in front of the TV; welcoming guests; or working on a Scout, 4-H, or "creative thinking" project. We

LOVE it, that's living! But when it's all over, there sits a four-foot stack of dishes, or a pile of muddy, grass-stained jerseys and sweatsuits. The rug is strewn with popcorn—greasy bowls everywhere, left lying where they were finished. Forgotten belongings (that will have to be boxed and mailed) and dirty sheets and towels are left after the visitors have said goodbye. Bits of pâpier-maché, beads, and feathers from kids' crafts are glued to the sun porch floor. And who is usually expected to deal with all this? A woman. Housework is hard work because it receives minor (if any) appreciation: All evidence of accomplishment is washed down the drain or chucked in the dumpster. **Housework for the most part isn't progressive, only restorative, getting back to where you started.** Where there is no glory, no status, no lasting evidence of achievement, it is only natural to dislike hard, drudging activity. It's not so much the physical work of housework, but the amount of a lifetime spent doing "invisible" things that embitters people. Doing the same chores over and over is discouraging. It's accepted that housework always "has to be done" and "somebody has to do it"—and we know who that "somebody" is. Constantly working hard just to be back where you started is not a fair burden to place on one person.

This can be changed by reducing the need to clean, designing work away, preventing dirt and junk from entering the house, getting a few professional secrets to cut corners—and above all, getting those who "dirty up" to clean up behind themselves. People can learn (before they go out on their own, when they'll *have* to) that housework isn't done by disembodied forces (*someone* has to deal with the stuff they drop in the hamper and forget).

Cleaning is everyone's job! Once they're out of diapers, anyone old enough to mess up is old enough to clean up. Cleaning is no more a woman's job than anyone else's, and

How Can I Clean to Reduce Allergies?

Many allergies (such as to dust, mold, animal dander, and certain chemicals) are directly related to cleaning, either the lack of it or the cleaning process itself. This is, of course, a highly individual matter. Some chronic allergy sufferers can sleep in a six-cat bed without problems, but they seize up at a whiff of the mildest cleaner. Others can't get within twenty feet of a pet, while the meanest cleaning odor or spray won't faze them.

No matter what your home circumstances, however, there are some standard safeguards that can reduce, control, and even prevent allergy problems:

1. Use mild, neutral cleaners whenever possible—avoid the strong ones. They may clean a bit faster and better but may also create or aggravate allergies.

2. Use methods that don't fill the air with cleaner mist, fog, or vapor—in other words, applying the solution with a sponge is better than spraying it all around. And don't work for any length of time in a confined area with strong cleaners. Provide good air circulation whenever you are using a strong cleaner or solvent.

3. Wear rubber gloves. Some of us can do all kinds of cleaning without gloves (without much more than a case of dry skin); others will instantly be in Rash City.

4. Buy and use the very best filter bags available for your vacuums, such as micro or hepa bags. They don't cost that much more, and they really reduce airborne irritants.

5. Be sure to have good filtration systems in your heating, cooling, and air circulation systems and machines, and service them regularly. The right kind of filters can catch a lot of dust, pollen, and mold spores.

6. Use good doormats at every home entrance, inside and out, and keep them clean so they can do their job.

7. Vacuum or dustmop rather than sweep, whenever you can.

8. If you're having a problem, limit the number of products you clean with so that you can more easily isolate the chemical or cleaning operation that causes a reaction.

9. Keep trash dumped—it always contains all kinds of dust and soils. If these are inside the house, they are still potential irritants.

10. Reduce those piles and stacks and stored hordes of unnecessary objects in key areas such as bedrooms. These things can harbor dust, dust mites, and mold spores—

especially things like old clothes, unused blankets, and fuzzy furnishings.

11. Choose laundry detergents carefully if you or your children have sensitive skin. Stick to dye-free and hypoallergenic detergents.

12. Frequently wash the bedding that is used by the allergy sufferer.

85

My Fiberglass Shower Is Impossible. How Do I Clean It?

Fiberglass, acrylics, and other plastic materials are now being used extensively to make inexpensive, lightweight tub and shower enclosures and shower doors. Builders often use these units because they are less costly than porcelain or ceramic tile units, and because they are easier to install. Unfortunately they often require more maintenance than the glazed finishes they have replaced, and are more easily damaged. With proper care, however, they can look good and be quite serviceable.

The basic thing to remember about fiberglass and plastic is to avoid damaging it, thereby making it more difficult to clean. Don't use abrasive cleaners or scouring pads, as these will roughen the surface and make the dirt cling harder. Strong oxidizers such as bleach, harsh acids, and volatile solvents can also damage the finish.

If you clean your fiberglass shower weekly, a mild acid bathroom cleaner should be used with a scrub pad that won't scratch, such as a white nylon or 3M's hourglass scrubber. For heavy hard water deposits, using it full strength is okay if you rinse it off right away. If soap scum is the problem, use a degreaser solution with a nonscratch scrub pad.

If you have a fiberglass unit that has been scoured and scratched, auto rubbing compound will polish it up again a little. The secret then is to keep it maintained—don't let mineral deposits and soap scum build up until cleaning is a major operation.

Try applying a silicone sealer such as Dazzle to a new shower (being careful to keep it off the floor of the tub or the shower) or to the old one after you've got it cleaned up. It repels spots and deposits and makes the unit easier to clean. Car wax can be used, too, but this can eventually lead to wax buildup that may have to be removed. Products containing wax or silicone (such as Dazzle, Armor All, or silicone glaze) should not be used on the floor unless you want to practice skiing in your shower.

86

How Do I Clean My Fireplace?

When home cleaners ask this question, they are usually refer-ring to the exterior face of the unit, not the firebox and inte-rior damper. A fireplace probably has more aesthetic appeal than energy or money-saving value, so those 95 percent of fireplaces with soot-blackened, grimy fronts cause owners not a little dis-comfort. Unsuccessful attempts to clean these often leave the face looking worse than before, and impossible to ever get clean, so be cautious.

My first advice about cleaning any fireplace is to vacuum it well with a dust brush attachment, then go over it with a dry sponge (see **Glossary** at the back of this book).

Before you baptize it with gallons of chemicals and liq-uids, check the surface. **(See pages 105–107 for how to clean brick.)** If your fireplace is constructed of light, soft sandstone or stark white unsealed brick, moisture will drive stains and dirt deeper into the surface. If the stone is an Oakley flagstone or other extremely hard nonporous masonry, then you can just get a bucket of degreaser solution and a good stiff-bristled brush and go at it. After the grime has all oozed out, spray-rinse with clear water (using a spray bottle or a common garden sprayer) and use some terry toweling to absorb the runoff. You can also use a wet/dry vac to suck water off brick or rock. If you have a soft, porous surface and a ten-year accumulation of crud, you

probably aren't going to get it sparkling clean, because time, humidity, and heat have already locked in the dirt film. Sometimes it's best to just leave it and call it rustic!

You could also sandblast it or paint it. Bricks painted with eggshell white enamel look sharp and can be cleaned easily.

Don't try to clean your brick fireplace with a bricklayer's muriatic acid bath (like your "expert" neighbor suggested). Acid baths are effective on new brick because they break down the chemical binders in any left-behind mortar drips, but on old dirty, greasy, dingy bricks they are relatively helpless. Half-cleaned bricks look worse than uncleaned ones. Muriatic acid, used carelessly, is also capable of damaging the mortaring. If mortar joints look bad, paint them with an opaque colored stain—it goes on quickly and accents the stone or brick nicely.

87

I've Cleaned Spots Out of My Carpet and Zap, They Reappear in the Same Place!

The return of spots is as frustrating as cutting weeds and having them pop up again. The solution to your carpet spot is the same as the way you keep weeds from reappearing. If you totally remove a weed, it won't return. If you get all the spot out of the carpet, no spot will return. **Spots "return" because of a process known as wicking.** Remember how a lamp wick moves kerosene up the wick to burn? Well, when most carpet spots are treated (only on the surface), the spot disappears, the carpet looks good, and the happy spotter leaves. Then moisture helps the stain residue deep in the carpet and backing "wick up" through the carpet fibers and dry on the top—and the carpet looks almost as bad as it did originally.

Any soap or cleaner residue left in a carpet after cleaning or spot removal leaves a sticky surface that attracts dirt; this is another reason "removed" spots reappear in the same place. Be sure to remove *all* the stain and *all* the soap residue when you clean up a spot. (See the stain removal steps and specific stain removers in my *Stainbuster's Bible*.) Remember, even if you can't see it, it's there, so keep working and absorbing and rinsing longer than you think you need to (that means flushing with fresh, clear water) until your clean white absorbing cloth shows no evidence of stain.

On carpet and upholstery, after it's cleaned, put a thick pad of toweling over the spot, weight it down with books, and leave it there for several hours to "wick up" any remaining moisture into the towel. This will help eliminate the reappearing "ring."

I Hear Warnings about Serious Accidents While Cleaning—How Could It Be Dangerous to Clean?

Nobody pays much attention to home accidents until they have one. Then they run around with a swollen eye, acid burns, or pinched fingers and spread scary tales. **More than half of all accidents happen in and around the home;** hundreds of thousands of them are directly connected with home cleaning or maintenance, because this is when people use unfamiliar chemicals, climb higher than they usually do, lift new and heavier objects, work when they are tired, or get so enthused with "progress" and getting finished that they forget to watch their step or where they set the paint bucket. Or forget to put dangerous chemicals out of the reach of children. I could tell you all sorts of gory stories, but a simple visual checklist might do a better job of preventing you from having to tell your own story of how you survived a ladder fall:

● Falls account for a high percentage of home accidents. Choosing stuff to stand on is no place to use your imagination—use only approved stepladders, stepstools, and scaffolding.

(Better yet, use an extension handle on your cleaning tool and avoid ladders altogether.)

When you do use a ladder, make sure it's set at a safe angle and firmly anchored. When you use a ladder, angle one foot from the wall for every four feet of height. Never stand on the top rung.

- Don't set the bucket at the foot of the ladder.
- Move the bucket *before* you move the ladder.
- Don't store stuff on the steps.
- To avoid slips and falls, rubber-soled shoes are the safest to use while cleaning. And you want shoes or sneakers, not bare feet or sandals that can catch in things or trip you up!
- Keep water away from electrical outlets or electrical anything.
- In the mood for a real shocker? Grab an old, frayed electrical cord with wet hands.

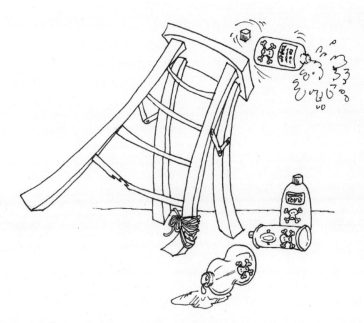

- Don't use damaged or ancient electric cords or extensions. Overloading electrical circuits is a major cause of fires.
- Get help lifting heavy objects. Next to falls, lifting injuries are the most common. If you have no help, move appliances and heavy furnishings the right way—with a cloth slipped underneath them.
- Sloppy storage can be dangerous. Be careful how you store and mix cleaning chemicals—many are caustic and poisonous.
- Wear safety glasses when using any dangerous chemical or solution that might splash on you, or when you do anything that means flying debris.
- Sweep it up—don't pick it up!
- Never reach under a beater-bar vacuum to see if the beater is working.
- Use rubber gloves when working with strong or harsh cleaners.
- Don't wring out mops with your hands—all mop heads pick up glass, pins, needles, toothpicks, and other sharp objects.

How Do I Clean Velvet Furniture?

What we call "velvet" today is likely to be plush or velour fabric, made of cotton, nylon, or acrylic, rather than the rayon, rayon/acetate, or even silk or wool of true or older velvet. Velvet and velour look great when new but are higher maintenance materials than most furniture covers.

The nap wear exaggerates worn spots, and any velvet or plush fabric (except crushed velvet) will look bad if portions of the nap become matted or lie or dry the wrong way. You can use a damp cloth to brush the nap up so it all stands uniform, but that's time-consuming.

To reduce wear on velvet or velour furniture, vacuum it often and turn and rotate the cushions every so often to even out the wear. To stave off the need for deep cleaning, spot clean it as necessary, the minute something is spilled or smeared on it. Use dry spotter (see **Glossary** at the back of this book) on a terry towel for greasy or oily stains. If a piece is an antique with true velvet, save the spot cleaning and any other cleaning for a professional.

Most furniture manufactured since 1969 carries a label with a code on it that indicates the kind of cleaning it can endure. "W" means water-based cleaners or spotters can be used, "S" means solvent cleaners only, "W-S" means either type is okay to use on it, and "X" means clean only by vacuuming or light brushing. On pieces marked W or W-S, spills should be

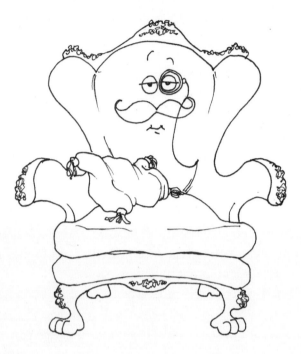

mopped up immediately, followed by a once-over with a cloth dampened with mild all-purpose cleaner solution, and then by a clean cloth wrung out in plain water. This cloth can also be used to smooth the nap back into the right direction. Heavily used areas like headrests and armrests can be wiped with the *foam only* of a good upholstery shampoo solution, left on there for a minute or two. Then blot the area with a clean towel and follow with a cloth dampened in clean water to rinse, and blot again.

Deep cleaning or "shampooing" of any type of velvet or velour furnishings is generally not a do-it-yourself project. Having them professionally dry-cleaned, or cleaned by an expert carpet cleaner, is the best way to go. Cotton velvet and velvet drapes of any kind should always be sent to the cleaners—let *them* sweat it.

Velvet is easier to enjoy in clothes than in furniture. (Which would you really rather have, a velvet chair to gaze upon or a snuggly velvet robe?) Bear this in mind when you're ogling that luxurious velvet love seat. **If you must go velvet, be sure to have soil retardant applied,** if it's an option, and remember that whites, yellows, and golds are tough to keep up; browns, reds, and greens help minimize problems.

90 ? ? ? ? ?

What Is the Best Way to Clean Shower Curtains?

If you've tried cleaning them in place (generally called the bathtub wrestling match) or laying them out on the rug or lawn (generally called stupid), you know that's not the way to go. Generously spray the area of the curtain that has soap scum

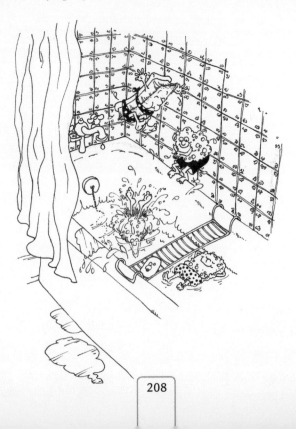

or hard water buildup with a bathroom cleaner designed to remove both hard water deposits and soap scum, such as my Non-Acid Bathroom Cleaner, and let it sit for five minutes or so. Then run the curtain through the washing machine on the warm, gentle setting.

There are a few kinds that you can't throw in your washer—check the label, or the washer after you're through, and the answer will be clear. **Remember that shower curtains are inexpensive, considering the amount of use they get—so consider replacement when they start looking shabby.**

Best of all is to eliminate shower curtains *and* shower doors, like I plan to do in my next low-maintenance house!

Should You Wash Walls and Ceilings Before Painting?

Only if they need it! The prime reason for cleaning before painting is to get paint to bond well to the old surface. Paint won't adhere well to dirt, grease, oil, cobwebs, spitballs, or sticky foodstuff-smeared walls, so most walls other than the pristine newly built should be cleaned in some way before painting.

If the wall or ceiling is greasy or grimy, wash it with a strong heavy-duty cleaner solution such as Super Orange. A wall with only mild age and wear can be dusted down and painted, or quickly swipe it down with a dry sponge. Stains and marks will probably be covered by the paint.

Some things that often do need to be removed are the specks, roller lint, and hair that stuck in the last coat of paint. You can't wash *that* off. A quick whish over the surface with fine sandpaper will have an amazing effect on the adherence and look of the finished job, especially on woodwork. If you are in doubt about some marks, such as felt-pen marks, ball-point pen ink, heavy black marks, and the like, slap a thin coat of clear shellac over them before painting, and let it dry—it will seal them off.

If cleaning seems impossible on some textures or in some situations, talk to your trusty paint store expert—there are special primers and sealers that can deal with just about any kind of surface.

92

Am I Lazy If I Hire Someone to Do My Cleaning?

Oddly, deciding whether or not to get outside help with the housework is often more of a "moral" than a financial issue. The question people who ask this are really asking is, "Do you think it's wrong to get someone else to do your cleaning?"

The answer is simple: no. It's great to get someone else to help around the house, if you need it. We all use professional help with the things we can't, won't, or don't want to do (such as driving, making clothes, or preparing food, among many others) Most of these things we could do ourselves, but for various reasons we find it more intelligent, economical, convenient, or satisfying to pay someone else to do them. Many of these things—which we delegate without a second thought every day and week of our lives—are no more skilled or personal than waxing floors, shampooing carpet, or cleaning high light fixtures.

Many people have physical conditions (such as allergies) or phobias (heights, noises, bugs, etc.) that make cleaning a horror. Many, too, have full-time or more jobs outside the home. Others entertain constantly and have ten times their share of cleaning. Sometimes even I have someone else clean my office because he does it well, has more time than I do, and needs a job. So I feel

good about it. Getting professional or outside help *is* the right, smart, and even admirable thing to do.

I'm a professional cleaner; that's what a maid, janitor, or other cleaning pro is. "We" do work when and where people can't justify or handle doing it themselves. We maids like to improve the mental as well as the physical quality of a home.

Once people use professional help, they usually find it is much more useful and far less expensive than membership in a spa or twenty extra gadgets on an automobile.

How Much Would It Cost to Have My Home Cleaned Professionally?

That depends on whether you own Dracula's castle, an 8' x 28' mobile home, or a studio apartment/condo. It also depends on what you define as "cleaned." I can give you a ballpark estimate on the two categories.

Cleaned I: Maid Work

Ordinary vacuuming, dusting, polishing, spot cleaning, sweeping, mopping, wax touchup, bathroom cleaning, watering plants, etc.:

Large Home	$55–$75 per time
Average Home	$50–$60 per time
Tiny Home	$35–$45 per time

If the cleaner uses his or her own equipment, add $5 per visit

Cleaned II: Professional Cleaning Crew

When a cleaning crew goes through the entire home, washing all walls, windows, and woodwork; waxing floors; shampooing carpet and upholstery:

5,000 sq. ft. big fancy home	$1,200 and up
4,000 sq. ft. big home	$900

1,800 sq. ft. average home $600
1,100 sq. ft. small home $400
800 sq. ft. average apartment $320

Average local travel costs and preparation time are already figured into these costs.

Variables

The state of the local labor market, age of the home and its general condition, type of furnishings, wall and floor coverings, amount of clutter in the home, number of knickknacks, whether or not the house has pets, etc., make a difference. Location makes a *big* difference. An average-size home seventy-five miles out in the desert from Las Vegas would probably cost more (considering travel time and vehicle use) than a big fancy home in the city would. Dusty weather conditions, hard water deposits on chrome and windows, and other environmental factors influence the cost too.

Get a bid! There are tons of pro cleaners, and the ones who know their business will know exactly what it will cost and can tell you to the penny. Then you can decide.

94

I Have Four Boys Who Miss the Toilet; What Should I Do?

Keep out of the way! Then **launch a consciousness-raising campaign**—most boys (and yes, men) guilty of this have never even stopped to think about or be aware of it.

Painting a red dot as a target near the bottom of the back of the toilet bowl will present an irresistible challenge. Signs that help create a hero-identification situation also help dry up careless behavior—Spiderman doesn't miss the toilet! And making them clean up their own mess with disinfectant cleaner solution—making sure they get around the base of the toilet as well as the floor area around it and any nearby surfaces—will improve accuracy 70 percent.

If that doesn't work, tell them if they're not careful, you might just grab and use their toothbrush to clean the floor around the base of the toilet next time.

Try these tactics and they should "aim to please"!

Why Won't My Kids Clean?

Most won't. There are several reasons for this, and if corrected, you might see them turn a hand.

They (like us) have too much. Probably 75 percent more toys than they need, for instance. Also clothes, tools, accessories, decorations. It's overwhelming!

Parents can set the wrong example. Kids watch and see one parent forever picking up after others and worrying about others' leavings and dirt. So they just join the crowd, usually letting Mom try to do it all.

✔ We order, send, or command them to clean, seldom teaching them how or, even more important, cleaning with them.

We unconsciously use cleaning as a punishment: "You little snots behave or you'll have to clean your room!" So they see it as a negative.

Peer performance. "Kelsey doesn't have to clean, why should I?"

Aside from maybe a stop to the nagging and yelling, what reward or consequence do they gain if they do it? Too often the answer is just use of the car, or some money. Maybe if they were convinced that we clean to feel good about ourselves and our surroundings, they would be more likely to rally to the cause.

With reading and other activities (and this goes for cleaning, too), the reward has to be in the thing itself—help your kids appreciate the satisfaction of a job well done when they pick up their toys or help create a leaf- and twig-free patio.

The real danger here (of constantly cleaning up behind them or letting them get away with not helping to clean the messes they make) is that **we are teaching them, at a very impressionable time, that they aren't responsible for their own messes.** So then when they are older and mess up financially, scholastically, spiritually, or in their jobs, big deal! It's somebody else's fault or job, they will think. The very thought of this is scary, so make those kids clean!

If I'm Going into Housecleaning Professionally, How Much Am I Worth?

I t all depends on how much work you can do in a given amount of time, in a professional manner. Certain jobs have a certain value, but your personal efficiency and technical skill are also important—how valuable you are will ultimately depend on how fast and well you can do the job. Most people could make $10–$30 per hour once they have gained true "professional status" in the housecleaning field. **True pro status comes through:**

1. **Experience:** Having faced and handled many different types of cleaning challenges—as well as the many types of *people* you have to deal with as a cleaner. Your confidence and competence will develop from experience.
2. **Study:** Seeking and reading written material, attending training sessions and seminars, keeping up with new products and methods will all help you be an efficient cleaner.
3. **Long hours of hard work:** A cleaning business is not a 9-to-5 job. You clean during "off" hours and lots of them. When competition keeps prices low, more hours of time have to be spent.

Don't work for an hourly wage; everyone is in the habit of thinking a cleaner ought to get minimum wage, and if you ask for an hourly rate higher than that, most customers' faces turn white. Instead, submit a bid for the work the customer has in mind. Tell the customer, "I'll wash all your windows and clean the blinds for $80." They like that because they know the cost, with no surprises; you can then work hard, fast, and efficiently, and do it in four hours and make $20 per hour. **You have to charge enough to cover more than your time.** Remember, you have the expenses of a phone, vehicle, gas, supplies, and equipment that will wear out. Occasionally you'll break or ruin something or even underbid a job or two.

Professional cleaning is a good direction to go, and here are some good places to inquire about cleaning career opportunities, professional training, sources of professional supplies, technique and material updates, etc. The following ought to be able to supply almost any cleaning information you want.

Building Service Contractors Association
10201 Lee Highway, Suite 225
Fairfax, VA 22030

Cleaning Management Institute
13 Century Hill Drive
Latham, NY 12110

Cleaning Center
P.O. Box 700-DV
Pocatello, ID 83204

Pick up a book called *Cleaning Up for a Living* from Betterway Books (I coauthored it with my Varsity associate Mark Browning). It has everything you need to know to run a successful cleaning operation, including a complete overview of the business, bidding, etc.

97

Is It Practical to Own Carpet-Shampooing Equipment?

Many people who own or rent a 3,000-square-foot or larger carpeted house or apartment figure they are in the big time and need to own some carpet-cleaning equipment. It looks practical on paper, because shampooing thousands of feet of carpet (at today's prices, twenty-five cents per square foot) can cost as much as $1,000 annually. For $800 to $1,500, you could get your own hot water extractor unit, which would last for years.

That sounds like it makes sense. But *first,* with good matting **(see page 97)** you won't have to shampoo as often. *Second,* if you watch for a professional carpet-cleaning sale, you can get your carpets cleaned for a surprisingly inexpensive "per-room" rate. *Third,* all this equipment (unit, hose, cord, wands, spotting kits, and so on) will take a heap of storage area. *Fourth,* **carpet extraction equipment is a high-maintenance item—it breaks and gets out of adjustment easily,** and will depreciate rapidly if not used and serviced regularly (and we aren't a service society anymore). *Fifth,* every neighbor, relative, friend, and carpet cleaner you know will find out that you have the unit and not only expect to borrow it, but feel slighted if you don't accompany it and do the job. (Borrowers are the true kiss of death to good carpet equipment.) *Sixth,* the carpet-cleaning chemical costs a lot, and also has to be picked up and

stored properly. *Seventh* is the work. The equipment looks neat and will do wonderful things, but running and lifting carpet equipment (and heaving furniture around) is gut-hard, skilled work—it requires not only a strong back but knowledge of color, fabrics and fibers, moisture control, spotting, etc. In a few cases where these factors don't bother you, it's a good idea.

✔ And no, don't think those handy-dandy home shampooers are the answer. They are less expensive and easier to handle but can't really do a professional job.

98

Don, Do You Help Your Wife Around the House?

I like to think I "run" things around our house. . . . Said "things" include, but are not limited to, the following: the vacuum cleaner, lawnmower, window squeegee, toilet plunger, carpet shampooer, paint roller, garbage compactor, waffle iron, mop bucket, brooms, sprinkler, dustcloth, etc. **I not only believe that men should be full partners in home cleaning, but I love to clean, so it's no problem at all.**

Although we keep things clean, we use our house hard and don't get excited if a fly dies in a window track. We live fairly simply—I think fancy cooking is a waste of time and overdecorated houses are a pain.

I also keep the house equipped with good tools, new efficient machines, and the best cleaning chemicals—the material and equipment necessary to minimize housework for all of us. I even bring in professionals from my company when extra help is needed, who seem to do a better job for my wife than they do for "The Boss."

How Do I Go about Dejunking a Home After Living There for Many Years—and Being a Pack Rat for Every One of Them?

Move! Have a sale, donate it all to charity, or (if the stuff was already old when you got it) open an antique shop! Don't love anything that can't love you back—that **JUNK is robbing you of tons of time and energy, and if you aren't using it, what good is it doing you?** It for sure isn't impressing or benefiting anyone.

Most junk served its purpose before it was salted away (like used gift wrap, dead wristwatches, old tires, worn faucets, old schoolbooks, and 1,000 more shelf-sitters)—you don't *really* need it, do you? Dejunking a home, office, or shop will do as much for you mentally as it will to save cleaning time. Every piece of junk stashed away or hidden (discreetly or indiscreetly) is also stashed away in your mind and is subconsciously taking a toll on your emotional, spiritual, and physical resources. Once discarded, it is discarded from your mind, and you are free from keeping mental tabs on it.

Another burden junk thrusts on us is that we feel obligated to use it whether we need it or not. If we don't use it, then we

worry about why we have it at all. Junk will get you—don't sit there and argue that it won't!

Recommended reading (in fact, the greatest stress-relieving gift you'll give to yourself all year):

Clutter's Last Stand, 2nd Edition (Adams Media)

The Office Clutter Cure, 2nd Edition (Adams Media)

Weekend Makeover: Take Your Home from Messy to Magnificent in Only 48 hours! (Adams Media)

Is It Worth It?

Sure it is! That's why you haven't given up before now. Although important, cleaning's number one value is not the removal of the physical dust, dirt, and disorder around us. It is the revitalization of our soul and spirit. Cleaning is one of the healthiest activities around, physically and mentally, because it improves our quality of life.

Clean is right up there when it comes to providing and creating good feelings. Clean, orderly surroundings just make us feel good. We can see clean, feel it, smell it, taste it. When things are picked up, we perk up! And clean things are much more pleasant to be around. What makes you feel better than "clean"—a clean slate or conscience, clean sheets, a clean shirt, sparkling windows, a newly vacuumed rug, or a freshly washed floor? And it's hard to beat the feeling of contentment and comfort we get from neatness and order.

And have you noticed that as you improve the speed and quality of your housework, other areas of your life seem to improve? It's called carryover. Cleaning and organizing a house is one of life's best seminars in self-improvement. You "absorb" more lessons than a sponge; you're uplifted even as you lift the grime from the garage floor.

The cleanliness level in your house projects your growing pride in yourself. The discipline and care with which you remove the dust and cobwebs from the corners of your rooms will carry over into a desire to wipe the cobwebs from the corners of your personality. One of housework's greatest values is its ability to build you into a more efficient, appealing person!

A clean house can and will get messed up again, but you can't mess up the improvements in quality of life your efforts have produced. How you live in and care for your dwelling shapes your personality—and your destiny. Home is the center of civilization. **It IS worth it!**

Glossary of Tools and Equipment

The tools talked about in this book are the tools the professionals use. I introduced them to home cleaners in 1981, and you couldn't tear them away now. It's easy to understand why. They do a faster and better job, and cost less in the long run, too.

Where can you get them? Where the pros do—at the janitorial-supply store. Just look in the Yellow Pages under "J," or do a Google search.

If you'd find it easier to order by mail from Don Aslett's Cleaning Center, send a postcard with your name and address to Clean Report, P.O. Box 700-DV, Pocatello, ID 83204, and we'll be happy to send you a catalog. Or, you can e-mail me at *don@aslett.com*.

Acid Cleaner

For removing mineral or "lime" scale. The 8 or 9 percent solution you can get at janitorial-supply stores (you don't want anything stronger than that for home use) will work much faster than supermarket delimers. See "Showers-n-Stuff."

All-Purpose Cleaner

A gentle but effective cleaner that will handle most of the household cleaning we do. Available as concentrate by the quart or gallon.

Bacteria/Enzyme Digester

A culture of live, beneficial bacteria that digest organic materials like vomit and urine that cause persistent and hard-to-remove stains and odors. Nilodor is one of my favorite brands.

Carpet Pretreat

A dirt- and grime-cutting solution such as Pre-Spray Carpet Treatment designed to be sprayed on traffic lanes and other heavily soiled areas of carpeting before shampooing, to help dissolve the dirt so the extractor can remove it.

Car-Washing Brush

A usually round brush on a long, hollow handle that can be attached to a garden hose so that you can scrub while you clean or rinse.

Cleaning Caddy

A sturdy, compartmentalized plastic container with a handle. It will store your cleaners and tools all together, neatly, so you don't waste time searching for them. Grab it and go—it's an easy way to keep your cleaning gear with you.

Cleaning Cloth

The pro cleaner's secret weapon, for quick streak-free drying, polishing, wiping, and mild scrubbing. Made from cotton terry cloth in 21" x 21" squares, or an ingenious design that gives you sixteen fresh surfaces to work with. Available from the Cleaning Center.

Compact Canister Vacuum

A vacuum such as Eureka's Mighty Mite is easy to carry and handle, yet has enough suction and capacity to do all of your above-the-floor vacuuming. Great for cleaning the car.

De-Solv-it

A citrus-oil solvent especially good for dissolving gum and adhesives. Sold in supermarkets, hardware stores, janitorial-supply stores, and the Cleaning Center.

Disinfectant Cleaner

A cleaner with serious germ-killing ability, for any place in the home that needs sanitizing or deodorizing. A "quaternary" is the kind you want. Concentrate is available in premeasured packets, quarts, or gallons.

Dry Sponge

A disposable 5" x 7" pad of soft rubber used to "dry clean" surface dirt and smoke from painted walls, paneling, ceilings, wallpaper, etc.

Dry Spotter

A solvent remover for oily stains that is safer than the old "dry cleaning fluid" that used to be sold for the purpose.

Dustmop

You want a 14" to 18" pro model with a cotton head and a swivel handle.

Dust Treat

Oily compounds applied to dustcloths and dustmops to help them attract and hold dust. Available as aerosols or liquids to put in your own spray bottle.

Extension Handle

Long, light, telescoping aluminum or fiberglass pole designed to be attached to cleaning tools (such as squeegees, dusters, even paint rollers) to extend your reach. A four-foot pole that extends to eight feet is a good size for home use.

Glass Cleaner

The pro version of a Windex-type cleaner you can mix up yourself inexpensively from concentrate. For spray cleaning small windowpanes, mirrors, appliances, chrome. Available in premeasured packets.

Grout Brush

A small brush that looks like a giant toothbrush, with stiff nylon bristles.

Heavy-Duty Cleaner/Degreaser

A meaner cleaner such as Soilmaster for when you're up against greasy or stubborn soil. Great as a laundry pretreat. Soil-master is a concentrate available by the quart or gallon. Heavy-duty cleaner is available in premeasured packets.

Hourglass Scrubber

A thin hourglass-shaped pad by 3M that can remove tough dirt without harming household surfaces, and reach corners and tight spaces easily.

Lambswool Duster

A large puff of wool on a long handle, which does high and low dusting with ease. You can also run it across detailed and convoluted surfaces like fancy picture frames, woodwork, and bookcases, and it will reach in and gently pull off the dust without disturbing anything. The natural oil and static attraction of the wool are the secret.

Masslinn Cloth

A disposable paper "cloth" that's chemically treated to catch and hold dust. It also leaves a nice nonoily low luster on furniture.

Mats

Professional "walkoff" mats for inside and outside the door. **Inside,** you want nylon or olefin pile with vinyl backing. **Outside,** you want something more textured, such as synthetic turf on a nonskid backing. Astroturf is my favorite outside mat. The bigger, the better—a good size is 3' x 4' or 3' x 5' or even 3' x 6'. There is a range of color choices in both indoor and outdoor walkoff mats.

Microfiber Cloth

Microfiber cleaning cloths have revolutionized cleaning around the house. They work wonders on every surface using plain water. Microfiber polishes mirrors and leaves no lint behind, it's great in the kitchen with greasy messes, and it even pulls spills out of carpets. Long-lasting economical cloths can be washed over and over again.

Mobile Cleaning Cart, Klean-GuRoo

A professional cleaning cart made especially for the home—a home cleaning center on wheels that holds everything you need to clean-as-you-go.

Nonacid Bathroom Cleaner

Designed to remove soap scum and alkaline soils. Use my Non-Acid Bathroom Cleaner for light hard water and scum removal. It won't mar fragile gold-tone finishes and is safe for marble or granite. For really tough problems in hard water areas, use my favorite, Showers-n-Stuff—it's a little more aggressive.

Oil Soap

A true soap (as opposed to the detergents we mostly clean with today) made from vegetable oil, such as Wood Wash. It's mild enough to clean wood surfaces safely, and the little bit of oil it leaves behind on the surface will be buffed by your drying towel to a handsome sheen.

Pet Rake

A tool specially designed to deal with the exasperating problem of pet hair everywhere. The crimped nylon bristles do an amazing job of getting it up and off upholstered furniture, bedding, car interiors, carpeting, and clothing. Available only from the Cleaning Center.

Rubber Broom

A broom with a telescoping handle and soft, short, flexible rubber bristles that capture hair, dust, and even the finest dirt. Turn it over, and you have a small floor squeegee. (Great for snow removal, too.)

Showers-n-Stuff

A blend of five acids plus detergent specially designed to remove not just soap and body oils, but the stubborn mineral deposits of hard water. Quickly removes mineral buildup from sinks, faucets, tubs, showers, and hard water–damaged windows.

Silicone Sealer

A silicone product, usually in a spray bottle, used to seal clean surfaces such as newly cleaned tile grout to help prevent resoiling. Also makes the treated surface slick and shiny so it can be cleaned more easily. My favorite brand is Dazzle.

Soil Retardant

A chemical applied to fabric and carpeting to make it soil and stain resistant, such as Scotchgard. Soil retardants usually need to be reapplied after deep cleaning.

Spray Bottle

Sturdy transparent plastic with a trigger-spray head. Pro-quality spray bottles perform better and last longer and come in quart size.

Squeegee

To do a first-class job of window cleaning, you need a pro-quality brass squeegee such as the Ettore. A 12" blade is best for most regular-size home windows; for picture windows and the like, you might want to go to 14" or larger.

Upright Vacuum

For speed, maneuverability, and pickup power on carpeting, these can't be beat. A commercial model such as the Windsor XP12 has a stronger motor, a beater bar, a disposable bag, a longer cord, and more durable and easily replaceable parts all over. It also has onboard tools.

"Wax" or Floor Finish

A professional quality self-polishing acrylic finish such as Top Gloss.

Wax Stripper

A strong cleaner and dissolvent designed for removing old wax from hard floors. Ask for a nonammoniated one. Our brand is called Mop Stripper.

White Nylon Scrub Sponge

A regular cellulose sponge on one side, white nylon mesh on the other. My all-around favorite cleaning tool. Enables you to get tough with dirt whenever you need to as you're cleaning along, without taking a chance of scratching things. 3M makes a good one.

X-O

An odor neutralizer, which eliminates bad odors by chemically canceling them out rather than just covering them up.

Zip-It

A long strip of plastic that you plunge down a drain, and as you pull it out the barbs pick up hair and other gunk that are clogging and slowing the drain. A Zip-It comes with a long narrow bag to put it in for easy, safe storage.

Full details on these and the whole universe of professional cleaning products can be found in *No Time to Clean!*, *The Cleaning Encyclopedia*, and *Is There Life After Housework?*

Index

List of Questions

Bonus Question!

Don, Why Do You Carry a Toilet Suitcase?

Doctors carry little black bags, lawyers and business executives carry attaché cases, and I carry a toilet suitcase because I'm a professional cleaner. The toilet, which I clean regularly (as do 10 million other professional cleaners and 100 million home cleaners), is a symbol of my trade. I carry it to dispel any doubt as to how I feel about my profession—I'm proud of it.

I'll admit, however, that when I meet a business contact and reach in my suitcase to get a business card, nobody will take it! And there's always a lot of suspense when it bumps out of the carousel at airports as people wait to see who will claim it.

More than forty-five years ago now, I started my cleaning career to pay for college. I put an ad in the local paper and homeowners began to call me. I shrank a few carpets and streaked walls and floors at first, but the homemakers whose homes I cleaned taught me as I went along. As I learned, I worked faster and developed new techniques for streamlining cleaning tasks—while still getting the job done right. I hired fellow students and named my growing company Varsity Contractors. Wanting to expand my business beyond homes, I landed a contract to clean the Bell Telephone building in our town—a big account! Today, Varsity Contractors is a multimillion-dollar business with offices in forty-seven states.

Not forgetting where I got my start, it was only natural that I try to repay the wonderful home cleaners who taught me the basics of cleaning. So, I began giving seminars to women's groups across the country, showing them how to use professional cleaning products and techniques to save up to 75 percent of the time they now spent on housework. I also wanted to help home cleaners be as proud of their profession as they should be.

I've been nicknamed by the media: "The Porcelain Preacher," "The Billy Graham of the Pine-Sol Set," "King of the Toilet Ring," "The Urinal Colonel," "Fastest Bowl Brush in the West," and "The Pied Piper of Purification." But I have the last laugh as I watch other businesspeople trying to balance attaché cases, coats, and umbrellas while trying to read newspapers. I just sit on my toilet suitcase and read my *Wall Street Journal!*

Don A. Aslett

For FREE information on:

How to order professional cleaning supplies

*How to sponsor a Don Aslett
speaking engagement in your area*

Don Aslett's schedule of appearances

Contact:
Don Aslett
P.O. Box 700-DV
Pocatello, ID 83204
E-mail: *don@aslett.com*

About the Author

As founder, owner, and chairman of the board of the multi-million-dollar facility services company, Varsity Contractors, Inc., Don Aslett has earned the well-deserved reputation as America's #1 cleaning expert. He is a favorite media celebrity and has taught thousands of seminars to audiences throughout the United States. Don is the author of more than two dozen books on cleaning, decluttering, and improving your personal and business productivity, which together have sold nearly three million copies.